Fodor's InFocus

CAYMAN ISLANDS

Excerpted from *Fodor's Caribbean*

14
TOP EXPERIENCES

The Cayman Islands offer terrific experiences that should be on every traveler's list. Here are Fodor's top picks for a memorable trip.

1 Seven Mile Beach

Those who love long, broad, uninterrupted sweeps of champagne-hued sand will be thrilled with Grand Cayman's longest beach. *(Ch. 6)*

2 Bird-watching on the Sister Islands

The Booby Pond on Little Cayman and the Brac's Parrot Reserve are just two of the gorgeous areas set aside for communing with nature. *(Ch. 7 & 8)*

3 Buying Crafts, Cayman Brac

Some of the best local crafts-people, including Annalee Ebanks (thatch-weaving) and Tenson Scott (caymanite carving), are found on the Brac. *(Ch. 7)*

4 George Town, Grand Cayman

In addition to dynamite duty-free shopping, the handsome waterfront capital hosts the historic Cayman Islands National Museum. *(Ch. 2)*

5 Pirates Point, Little Cayman

The dinners here aren't quite as elegant or complex as what you might find at one of Grand Cayman's top spots, but the bon mots and bonhomie are unmatched. *(Ch. 8)*

6 Queen Elizabeth II Botanic Garden

Critically endangered blue iguanas have found a home at this park, where you learn about their life cycles, then stroll the peaceful, gorgeously laid-out gardens. *(Ch. 2)*

7 Stingray City, Grand Cayman

You can interact with gracefully balletic, silken stingrays, so "tame" you can feed them as they beg for handouts on this shallow sandbar in the North Sound. *(Ch. 6)*

8 Diving Bloody Bay Wall

One of the top dive sites in the world plunges from 18 feet to more than a mile into the Cayman Trench; the visibility is remarkable. *(Ch. 6)*

9 Barefoot Man at the Reef Resort

Head to Pelican's Reef on the East End of Grand Cayman to hear the blond Calypsonian, Barefoot Man (née George Nowak), a beloved island icon. *(Ch. 5)*

10 Happy Hour, Grand Cayman

Such popular waterfront spots as Rackam's and The Wharf serve creative cocktails and reel in the revelers for sunset tarpon feeding. *(Ch. 5)*

11 Owen Island, off Little Cayman

Easily accessible by kayak from Little Cayman's "mainland," Owen Island appeals to snorkelers and romantics, who have their choice of captivating coves. *(Ch. 8)*

12 Local Food, Grand Cayman

Sample mouth- and eye-watering jerk chicken from a roadside stall or George Town shack. A few local chefs even serve meals in their homes. *(Ch. 3)*

13 Blue by Eric Ripert, at the Ritz-Carlton

The wine-pairing menu at Le Bernardin chef Eric Ripert's only Caribbean restaurant is the kind of epicurean experience that comes along once in a blue moon. *(Ch. 3)*

14 Underwater Sculpture, Cayman Brac

Nature's artistry is matched by the world's largest (and still growing) underwater installation, the sculptor Foots's gorgeously imagined, impressively engineered Lost City of Atlantis. *(Ch. 7)*

CONTENTS

ABOUT THIS GUIDE

Fodor's Ratings

Everything in this guide is worth doing—we don't cover what isn't—but exceptional sights, hotels, and restaurants are recognized with additional accolades. Fodor's Choice ★ indicates our top recommendations; ★ highlights places we deem highly recommended. Care to nominate a new place? Visit Fodors.com/contact-us.

Trip Costs

We list prices wherever possible to help you budget well. Hotel and restaurant price categories from $ to $$$$ are noted alongside each recommendation. For hotels, we include the lowest cost of a standard double room in high season. For restaurants, we cite the average price of a main course at dinner or, if dinner isn't served, at lunch. For attractions, we always list adult admission fees; discounts are usually available for children, students, and senior citizens.

Hotels

Our local writers vet every hotel to recommend the best overnights in each price category, from budget to expensive. Unless otherwise specified, you can expect private bath, phone, and TV in your room. For expanded hotel reviews, facilities, and deals visit Fodors.com.

Restaurants

Unless we state otherwise, restaurants are open for lunch and dinner daily. We mention dress code only when there's a specific requirement and reservations only when they're essential or not accepted. To make restaurant reservations, visit Fodors.com.

Credit Cards

The hotels and restaurants in this guide typically accept credit cards. If not, we'll say so.

Top Picks					
★ Fodor's Choice		⊡	Admission fee	✕	Restaurant
		⊙	Open/closed times	⌂	Reservations
Listings				🏛	Dress code
⊠	Address	Ⓜ	Subway	⊟	No credit cards
⊠	Branch address	↔	Directions or Map coordinates	⑤	Price
⌨	Mailing address				
☎	Telephone	**Hotels & Restaurants**		**Other**	
⊟	Fax			⇨	See also
⊕	Website	⊡	Hotel	☞	Take note
✎	E-mail	⌂	Number of rooms	🏌	Golf facilities
		⑩	Meal plans		

DID YOU KNOW?

The endangered Lesser Cayman's iguana that is endemic to Little Cayman and Cayman Brac was recently introduced in Grand Cayman.

EXPERIENCE THE CAYMAN ISLANDS

WHAT'S WHERE

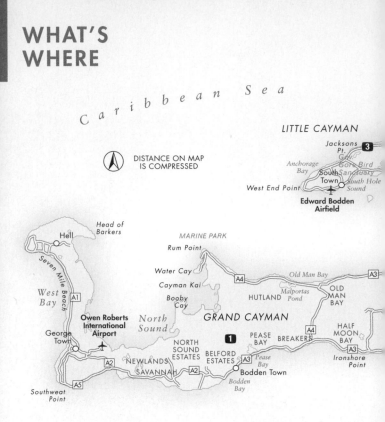

Caribbean Sea

DISTANCE ON MAP
IS COMPRESSED

LITTLE CAYMAN

Jacksons Pt. **3**
Gore Bird
Anchorage Bay South Sanctuary
Town South Hole
West End Point Sound
Edward Bodden Airfield

Head of Barkers

Hell

MARINE PARK
Rum Point

Seven Mile Beach

Water Cay Old Man Bay A3

West Bay A1 Cayman Kai A4 OLD MAN BAY
Booby Cay HUTLAND Malportas Pond

Owen Roberts International Airport *North Sound* GRAND CAYMAN HALF MOON BAY

George Town PEASE BAY BREAKERS A4
NORTH SOUND ESTATES BELFORD ESTATES A3 A3
A2 NEWLANDS *Pease Bay* Ironshore Point
SAVANNAH A2 Bodden Town

A5

Southweat Point *Bodden Bay*

1 **Grand Cayman.** The Cayman Islands' main island offers the longest, liveliest sandy strand (Seven Mile Beach), great diving, fine dining, upscale resorts, surprisingly varied nightlife, and an attractive waterfront capital with duty-free shopping in George Town. Despite the development and congestion around Seven Mile Beach and George Town, the neighborhoods of West Bay and East End are mellow and filled with natural wonders.

2 **Cayman Brac.** The archipelago's most rugged, dramatically scenic island is known for its bullying bluff, which vaults 140 feet. The bird-watching, caving, hiking, and rock climbing (experienced only with your own gear) are phenomenal, and the island is just as spectacular underwater for divers and snorkelers. The Brac is laid back, friendly, and cheap, with good villa values and small inns and resorts.

Booby
Pt. North East
Pt.
North East Bay
Tibbetts Turn
Spot
Bay
Stake Bay Pt.
Deadman's Pt.
Pollard
Bay
Lower Spot
Bay
Crawl
Bay
East Point
Cat Head Bay
Frenchman's
Fort
Tom Jennett's Bay
Sea Feather Bay
West End
Charles Bight
West End Pt.
Gerrard-Smith
Airport
Cedar Pt.
CAYMAN BRAC

Spotter Bay
COLLIERS
Colliers Bay
EAST
END
Lower
Bay

The Bahamas
ATLANTIC OCEAN
Cuba
Dominican
Republic
Haiti
Caribbean Sea
COLOMBIA
VENEZUELA
Caribbean

3 Little Cayman. The smallest of the Cayman Islands is the least developed, most unspoiled in the chain. Ecotourists can get back to nature (but not the basics) at splendid little resorts catering to divers and birders. You'll find world-famous dive sites like Bloody Bay Marine Park, equally fantastic fishing (especially light-tackle), secluded beaches, and fabulous bird-watching along the shore and wetlands covering nearly half the island.

PLANNER

Island Activities	Logistics
Diving is a major draw; the Bloody Bay Wall, off the coast of Little Cayman, is one of the Caribbean's top dive destinations, but there are many sites convenient to Grand Cayman where shore diving is also good.	**Getting to the Islands:** There are plenty of nonstop flights to Grand Cayman (GCM) from the United States; then you can hop over to the Brac (CYB) and Little Cayman (LYB) on a small plane.
On Grand Cayman, a dive or snorkeling trip to **Stingray City** is very popular. There's good off-the-beach snorkeling in West Bay Cemetery, at Rum Point, and at Smith's Cove in Grand Cayman.	**Hassle Factor:** Low for Grand Cayman; medium to high for Little Cayman and Cayman Brac.
On land, Grand Cayman has the most to offer, with plenty of tours and activities, including **semisubmersible tours** of the bay.	**Nonstops:** You can fly nonstop to Grand Cayman from Atlanta (Delta, three times weekly), Boston (US Airways and JetBlue once weekly), Charlotte (US Airways), Detroit (Delta once weekly), Fort Lauderdale (Cayman Airways), Houston (United once weekly), Miami (American, Cayman Airways), Minneapolis (Delta once weekly), New York–JFK (Cayman Airways daily, JetBlue three times weekly, Delta once weekly), New York–Newark (United once weekly), Philadelphia (US Airways once weekly), and Tampa (Cayman Airways).
Grand Cayman's **Seven Mile Beach** is one of the Caribbean's finest long stretches of sand. Little Cayman has the best beaches of the Sister Islands, especially Owen Island and Point o' Sand.	**On the Ground:** In Grand Cayman you must take a taxi or rent a car at the airport, since most hotels are not permitted to offer airport shuttles. Hotel pickup is more readily available on Cayman Brac and Little Cayman.
Rock climbers have now discovered the Brac's limestone bluff.	**Renting a Car:** It's possible to get by without a car on Grand Cayman if you are staying in the Seven Mile Beach area. If you want to explore the rest of the island—or if you are staying elsewhere—you'll need a car. Though less necessary on Cayman Brac or Little Cayman, cars are available on both islands. Driving is on the left, and you need a local driving permit, available at the car-rental office for US$20.

Where to Stay

Grand Cayman is expensive during the high season but offers the widest range of resorts, restaurants, and activities. Both Little Cayman and Cayman Brac are more geared toward serving the needs of divers, who compose the majority of visitors. The smaller islands are cheaper than Grand Cayman, but with the extra cost of transportation, the overall savings are minimized.

Grand Cayman: Grand Cayman has plenty of medium-size resorts as well as the Ritz-Carlton, a large seven-story resort on Seven Mile Beach. The island also has a wide range of condos and villas, many in resortlike compounds on or near Seven Mile Beach and the Cayman Kai area. There are even a few small guesthouses for budget-minded visitors.

The Sister Islands: Cayman Brac has mostly intimate resorts and family-run inns. Little Cayman has a mix of small resorts and condos, most appealing to divers.

Hotel and Restaurant Costs

Prices in the restaurant reviews are the average cost of a main course at dinner or, if dinner is not served, at lunch; taxes and service charges are generally included. Prices in the hotel reviews are the lowest cost of a standard double room in high season, excluding taxes, service charges, and meal plans (except at all-inclusives). Prices for rentals are the lowest per-night cost for a one-bedroom unit in high season.

Tips for Travelers

1

All visitors must have a valid passport and a return or ongoing ticket to enter the Cayman Islands.

The minimum legal drinking age in the Cayman Islands is 18.

Electricity is reliable and is the same as in the United States (110 volts/60 cycles). U.S. electrical appliances will work just as if at home.

You should not need to change money in Grand Cayman, since U.S. dollars are readily accepted. ATMs generally offer the option of U.S. or Cayman dollars. The Cayman dollar is pegged to the U.S. dollar at the rate of approximately CI$1.25 to $1. Be sure you know which currency is being quoted when making a purchase.

IF YOU LIKE

Getting Away from It All

Though Grand Cayman's Seven Mile Beach is completely developed, other areas of the island still offer respite from the crowds as do the Sister Islands. Here are some ideas for romantic R&R:

Cotton Tree, Grand Cayman. This serene West Bay sanctuary artfully combines Cayman heritage with a gaggle of the latest gadgets and other luxe amenities.

Pirates Point and The Southern Cross Club, Little Cayman. You can't go wrong with either of Little Cayman's upscale yet down-home intimate beachfront resorts.

Lighthouse Point, Grand Cayman. This ecocentric hideaway recycles practically everything, allowing guests to get back to nature but not the basics.

Cayman Breakers, Cayman Brac. Tucked away at the remotest point on the Brac, this condo complex satisfies any desire for seclusion; the owners have built an even more elegant complex next door.

The Reef, Grand Cayman. If you crave activity and facilities galore, yet still value privacy, this midsize resort fits the bill on Grand Cayman's East End.

Great Eating

Foodies can savor a smorgasbord of gastronomic goodies, from sophisticated fusion fare to fiery local cuisine—and everything in between. Try these special spots:

Blue by Eric Ripert, Grand Cayman. Ripert's great NYC seafood-centric eatery, Le Bernardin, goes coastal with shipshape results.

Michael's Genuine Food & Drink, Grand Cayman. James Beard Award–winning chef Michael Schwartz delectably adapts his Miami outpost's "slow food" philosophy.

Mizu, Grand Cayman. This popular pan-Asian eatery exudes sex appeal, whether it's the decor, the waitstaff, or the sensuously textured preparations.

Ortanique, Grand Cayman. Celebrity chef Cindy Hutson and her partner Delius Shirley make waves with this outpost of their Floribbean sensation.

Morgan's Harbour, Grand Cayman. Enjoy the stellar views of fishing dinghies and pleasure craft cruising the North Sound alongside pub grub elevated to an art form.

Cimboco, Grand Cayman. Everything about this spot is creative, from the boldly colored decor to the innovative takes on Caribbean cuisine.

Pirate's Point, Little Cayman. It's practically worth a day trip from Grand Cayman to enjoy the food

and conversation at Gladys Howard's lovely retreat.

The Water

Bloody Bay and Stingray City are the showcase attractions in Cayman, but here are some suggestions for other stellar sites as well as aquatic activities aplenty:

Wreck Diving, Grand Cayman and Cayman Brac. The Cayman Islands government sank the decommissioned 251-foot USS *Kittiwake* to create another artificial reef, while the Brac counters with the 330-foot *Capt. Keith Tibbetts*, a virtual fireworks display of reel life.

Shore Diving, Grand Cayman. Silverside minnows swarm in the grottoes at Eden Rock, forming liquid silver lamé curtains of fish; its neighbor, the Devil's Grotto, resembles an abstract marine painting.

Kayaking, Grand Cayman. Glide through protected mangrove wetlands teeming with a unique ecosystem; the Bio Bay tour on moonless nights is unforgettable.

Deep See Cayman, Grand Cayman. To explore the underwater world without getting your feet wet, Deep See Cayman uses a robot to plumb the depths up to 2,400 feet, transmitting live feed as you watch on a yacht.

Sportfishing, Cayman Brac and Little Cayman. Both Sister Islands offer sensational bonefishing in the flats, as well as deep-sea fishing for marlin, wahoo, and sushi-grade tuna.

Shopping

It's fun to bring home a memento for yourself and souvenirs for your friends and family. Here are some suggestions:

Caymanian Crafts, Grand Cayman and Cayman Brac. The Cayman Craft Market and fun funky stores like Pure Art sell everything from local preserves to paintings, while Tenson Scott on the Brac is famed for his Caymanite creations.

Rum and More Rum, Grand Cayman. Cayman's own Seven Fathoms Rum produces a mellow spirit via a unique underwater aging process, while Tortuga Rum is celebrated for its rum-soaked cakes in many flavors.

Art, Grand Cayman. Find original paintings and sculptures by Cayman artists, including Al Ebanks, Luelan Bodden, Gordon Solomon, Nickola McCoy-Snell, and Randy and Nasaria Suckoo Cholette.

Jewelry, Grand Cayman. Downtown George Town is practically one giant duty-free shopping center, highlighting numerous name brands and individual jewelers, while conspicuous consumption continues in the malls along Seven Mile Beach.

WHEN TO GO

The high season in the Cayman Islands is traditionally winter—from December 15 to April 15—when northern weather is at its worst. It's the most fashionable, the most expensive, and the most popular time to visit—and most resorts are heavily booked. You must make reservations at least two or three months in advance for the very best places (sometimes a year in advance for the most exclusive spots). Hotel prices drop 20%–50% after April 15; airfares and cruise prices also fall. Saving money isn't the only reason to visit the Cayman Islands during the off-season. In summer the sea is even calmer (ideal for diving—except when tropical storms roil the waters), and things move at a slower pace. The water is clearer for snorkeling and smoother for sailing in May, June, and July, when the big game fish, though abundant year-round, really run riot.

Climate

The average daily temperature is about 80°F, and there isn't much variation from the coolest to the warmest months, including the water temperature. Rainfall averages 50 to 60 inches per year (less in the more arid Sister Islands and Grand Cayman's East End). But in the tropics, rainstorms tend to be sudden and brief, often erupting early in the morning and at dusk. Toward the end of summer, hurricane season begins in earnest. Starting in June, islanders pay close attention to the tropical waves as they form and travel across the Atlantic from Africa. In an odd paradox, tropical storms passing by leave behind the sunniest and clearest days you'll ever see.

Festivals and Events

January gets the Cayman calendar literally cooking with the celebrity-heavy **Cayman Cookout** co-organized by top toque Eric Ripert, followed by Taste of Cayman in February. February also usually celebrates Cayman culture in the **Arts Festival.** Cayman explodes with color every April with its take on Carnival called **Batabano.** May's **Cayman Islands International Fishing Tournament** lures anglers from around the world. November's **GimiSTORY** celebrates Cayman's rich oral storytelling tradition. But the big blockbuster is November's **Pirates Week Festival,** when Grand Cayman turns into one giant 11-day party, featuring parades, costume competitions, street dances, Heritage Days, mock pirate invasions, sporting events, fireworks, and delicious local grub.

GREAT ITINERARIES

It's a shame that so few visitors (other than divers) spend time on more than one island in a single trip. If you have more than a week, you can certainly spend some quality time on both Grand Cayman and one of its Sister Islands.

If You Have 3 Days

Ensconce yourself at a resort along Grand Cayman's **Seven Mile Beach,** spending your first day luxuriating on the sand. On Day 2, get your feet wet, if you snorkel or dive, at **Stingray City and Sandbar** in West Bay, where you can feed the alien-looking gliders by hand. Splurge for a great dinner on your second night, perhaps at **Blue by Eric Ripert.** On your last day, head into **George Town** for some shopping. Have lunch with scintillating harbor views at **Breezes by the Bay** or **Casanova** before soaking up some last rays of sun.

If You Have 7 Days

Since divers need to decompress before their return flight, the last day should be spent sightseeing on Grand Cayman. **The Cayman Turtle Farm,** the expensive but exceptional marine theme park, is a fine destination. On the East End you could hike the pristine **Mastic Trail,** then stroll through the gorgeous grounds at **Queen Elizabeth II Botanic Park.** Spend your final morning in George Town (perhaps snorkeling **Eden Rock**). Non-div-ers, too, should explore a bit farther afield instead of spending all their time at Seven Mile Beach. A full day around West Bay, perhaps beachcombing at savagely beautiful **Barkers,** is a good choice. If you have a car, explore the East End natural attractions, lunching at the **Lighthouse.** Head east another day to visit historic **Pedro St. James Castle;** drive through the original capital, **Bodden Town;** then spend the afternoon (lunch, swimming, and water sports) at **Cayman Kai/ Rum Point.**

If You Have 10 Days

With 10 days, you can spend time on two or even all three islands. Begin on Cayman Brac; after diving the **north coast** walls, **MV *Capt. Keith Tibbetts,*** and the **Lost City of Atlantis** (or just lying on the beach), save a morning to hike through the **Parrot Reserve,** perhaps out to the **East End Lighthouse** for its sensational views (or climb the Lighthouse Steps, peeking into **Peter's Cave**). On Little Cayman, chill out picnicking on **Owen Island,** and don't miss the **Booby Pond Nature Reserve.** Spend at least two nights on Grand Cayman.

WEDDINGS AND HONEYMOONS

There's no question that the Cayman Islands, especially Grand Cayman, are one of the Caribbean's foremost honeymoon destinations. Destination weddings are also particularly popular on Grand Cayman, where the larger resorts have wedding planners to help you with the paperwork and details.

The Big Day

Choosing the Perfect Place. When choosing a location, remember that you really have two choices to make: the ceremony location and the reception location. For the former, there are beaches, bluffs overlooking beaches, gardens, private residences, historic buildings, resort lawns, and, of course, places of worship (after which you can trot away to your life together in a horse-drawn carriage). Most couples choose to say their vows on lovely Seven Mile Beach, with the sun setting into the azure sea as their picture-perfect backdrop. Underwater weddings in full scuba gear with schools of fish as impromptu witnesses are also possible (kissing with mask on optional). Cathy Church can photograph your underwater wedding *(see ⇨ Shopping in Chapter 2)*. You can literally leave things up in the air, getting hitched while hovering in a helicopter ("I do; Roger and out," responded one blushing bride over the propeller noise). As for the reception, you can opt for most of the same choices, as well as restaurants. If you decide to go outdoors, remember the seasons—yes, the Caribbean has seasons. If you're planning a wedding outdoors, be sure you have a backup plan in case it rains. Also, if you're planning an outdoor wedding at sunset—which is very popular—be sure you match the time of your ceremony to the time the sun sets at that time of year.

Finding a Wedding Planner. If you're planning to invite more than a minister and your loved one to your wedding ceremony, seriously consider an on-island wedding planner, who can help select a location, help design the floral scheme and recommend a florist as well as a photographer, help plan the menu, and suggest any local traditions to incorporate into your ceremony.

Of course, all the larger resorts have their own wedding planners on-site. If you're planning a resort wedding, work with the on-site wedding coordinator to prepare a detailed list of the exact services he or she will provide. If your idea of your wedding doesn't match the resort's services, try a different resort. Or look for independent wedding planners, who do not work directly for resorts.

Legal Requirements. Documentation can be prepared ahead of time or in one day while on the

island. A minimal residency waiting period, blood test, and shots aren't required.

You need to supply a Cayman Islands international embarkation/disembarkation card, as well as proof of identity (a passport or certified copy of your birth certificate signed by a notary public), and age (those under 18 must provide parental consent). If you've been married before, you must provide proof of divorce with the original or certified copy of the divorce decree if applicable or a copy of the death certificate if your previous spouse died. You must list a marriage officer on the application, and you need at least two witnesses; if you haven't come with friends or family, the marriage officer can help you with that, too. A marriage license costs CI$200 (US$250).

Wedding Attire. In the Caribbean, basically anything goes, from long, formal dresses with trains to white bikinis. Floral sundresses are fine, too. Men can wear tuxedos or a simple pair of solid-color slacks with a nice white linen shirt. If you want formal dress and tuxedo, it's usually better to bring your formal attire with you.

Photographs. Deciding whether to use the photographer supplied by your resort or an independent photographer is an important choice. Resorts that host a lot of weddings usually have their own photographers, but you can also find independent, professional island-based photographers, and an independent wedding planner will know the best in the area. Look at the portfolio (many photographers now have websites), and decide if this person can give you the kind of memories you are looking for. If you're satisfied with the photographer that your resort uses, make sure you see proofs and order prints before you leave the island.

The Honeymoon

Do you want champagne and strawberries delivered to your room each morning? A maze of a swimming pool in which to float? A five-star restaurant in which to dine? Then a resort is the way to go, and Grand Cayman offers options in different price ranges. Whether you want a luxurious experience or a more modest one, you'll certainly find someplace romantic to which you can escape. You can usually stay on at the resort where your wedding was held. On the other hand, maybe you want your own private home in which to romp naked—or maybe your own kitchen in which to whip up a gourmet meal for your loved one. In that case, a private vacation-rental home or condo is the answer.

KIDS AND FAMILIES

Grand Cayman and, to a much lesser extent, Cayman Brac jump with activities and attractions that will keep children of all ages (and their parents) happily occupied. Some resorts and hotels welcome children, others do not, and still others restrict kids to off-season visits. All but the fanciest (and most expensive) restaurants are kid-friendly.

Family-Friendly Resorts

The **Ritz-Carlton,** the biggest and most fashionable of the island's resorts, welcomes children at any time with "edu-tainment" programs for all ages, including Jean-Michel Cousteau's Ambassadors of the Environment initiative introducing Cayman's culture and ecology. Less pricey is **Grand Cayman Marriott Beach Resort** on Seven Mile Beach with children's programs and a fine stretch of beach. Many of the condo complexes toward the northern end of Seven Mile Beach, such as **Christopher Columbus** and **Discovery Point Club,** offer good value and a wide rock-free strand. On Cayman Brac, the **Brac Reef Beach Resort** is best equipped for families. Little Cayman is too quiet for most kids, but the **Little Cayman Beach Resort** can keep children occupied while their parents dive.

Family-Friendly Dining and Activities

Dining out with the family is not an issue, as Grand Cayman has more restaurants than you can count serving a virtual United Nations of cuisines. The Sister Islands are much more limited in their offerings, though the friendly locals will do their utmost to please finicky palates. **Camana Bay** is definitely family-friendly, from climbing the Observation Tower for smashing panoramas to splashing in the fountains and watching the frequent street performers. Most of the islands' water-based activities cater to kids, including **Deep See Cayman, the Atlantis semisubmersible, Stingray City snorkeling tours,** and the **Dolphin Discovery.** The attractions at the **Cayman Turtle Farm,** including the predator reef and breeding facility, mesmerize all ages, as will learning about blue iguanas at their habitat in the **Queen Elizabeth II Botanical Garden.** Pipes, ramps, and rails galore, not to mention a wave-surf machine, have kids screaming while doing wheelies at the **Black Pearl Skate & Surf Park.**

EXPLORING GRAND CAYMAN

With Shopping

By Jordan
Simon

Though Grand Cayman is most celebrated for its aquatic activities, there's no shortage of diversions to please land-lubbers, history buffs, the ecocentric, and families, from turtle and butterfly farms to ruined fortifications. It's just as alluring on land as underwater, gleaming with a ravishing dryness. Though not lush, the surrounding scenery can spiral from arid semidesert to tropical hardwood forests that pierce the sky like cathedral spires. Many attractions admirably attempt to foster greater understanding of the environment and the importance of responsible stewardship of our resources.

Window-shopping in the captivating capital, George Town, ranks as many visitors' favorite form of recreation and sightseeing. Not only will you find no additional sales tax, but there's duty-free merchandise aplenty. And though most people's image of Grand Cayman is bustling Seven Mile Beach, there are downright rural, pastoral pockets where if time doesn't stand still, it slows to a turtle's steady crawl. This is where travelers can experience the "real" Cayman, including craft traditions such as thatch weaving that have nearly vanished.

EXPLORING GRAND CAYMAN

The historic capital of George Town, on the southeast corner of Grand Cayman, is easy to explore on foot. If you're a shopper, you can spend days here; otherwise, an hour will suffice for a tour of the downtown area. To see the rest of the island, rent a car or scooter or take a guided tour. The portion of the island called West Bay is noted for its jumble of neighborhoods, many featuring ornate Edwardian homes built by seafarers, nautical tour companies (and real fishing fleet) at Morgan's Harbour, and a few attractions. When traffic is heavy, it's about a half hour to West Bay from George Town, even with the newer bypass road that runs parallel to West Bay Road. The less-developed North Side and East End have natural attractions from blowholes to botanical gardens, as well as the remains of the island's original settlements. Plan on at least 45 minutes for the drive out from George Town (more than an hour during rush hours). You need a day to explore the entire island—including a stop at a beach for a picnic or swim.

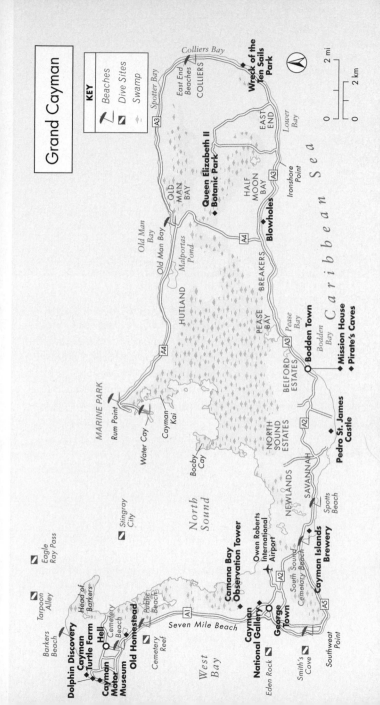

Grand Cayman

KEY
- Beaches
- Dive Sites
- Swamp

An aerial view of West Bay

CRUISE CRUSH. On certain days George Town, Seven Mile Beach, and even West Bay's attractions crawl with cruise-ship hordes. Check the Cayman Island Port Authority (⊕ *www.caymanport. com/shipschedules.ptp*) for the latest schedule and plan accordingly, unless you like being trampled. There may be anywhere from one to three ships at anchor off George Town any day of the week, but more ships tend to call on Tuesday, Wednesday, and Thursday.

GEORGE TOWN

Begin exploring the capital by strolling along the waterfront, Harbour Drive, to **Elmslie Memorial United Church**, named after the first Presbyterian missionary to serve in the Caymans. Its vaulted timber ceiling (built from salvaged wreck material in the shape of an upside-down hull), wooden arches, mahogany pews, and tranquil nave reflect the island's deeply religious nature.

Just north near Fort Street, the **Seamen's Memorial Monument** lists 153 names on an old navigational beacon; a bronze piece by Canadian sculptor Simon Morris, titled *Tradition*, honors the almost 500 Caymanians who have lost their lives at sea. Dive-industry pioneer Bob Soto, wife Suzy, and daughter-in-law Leslie Bergstrom spearheaded

2

BEST BETS

- **Feeling Blue.** Visiting the endangered blue iguana compound at the glorious Queen Elizabeth II Botanic Park.

- **Petting a Turtle.** Though it's hideously expensive, the Turtle Farm encapsulates everything that makes Cayman special. And admission to its world-class turtle research center/farm, true edu-tain-ment, is cheaper.

- **Getting Touched by History.** Pedro St. James Castle bears eloquent testimony to Caymanian struggles for democracy, freedom, and survival against the elements.

- **National Trust–worthy.** The National Trust is an admirable institution dedicated to preserving the Caymanian environment and culture. If you're on island when they're running a tour (perhaps to the bat caves or historic homes) or a demonstration (cooking, thatch weaving), go!

- **Whatta Guy.** When he's not off adventuring, acclaimed marine biologist-artist Guy Harvey is usually in his amazing gallery-shop; buy a print, ask him to sign it, and converse on conservation.

the project, which Prince Edward unveiled during the 2003 quincentennial celebrations.

A few steps away lie the scant remains of **Fort George,** constructed in 1790 to repel plundering pirates; it also functioned as a watch post during World War II to scan for German subs.

In front of the court building, in the center of town, names of influential Caymanians are inscribed on the **Wall of History,** which also commemorates the islands' quincentennial. Across the street is the Cayman Islands **Legislative Assembly Building,** next door to the **1919 Peace Memorial Building.** A block south is the horseshoe-shaped **General Post Office,** built in 1939 at the tail end of the art deco period. Let the kids pet the big blue iguana statues.

★ Fodor'sChoice **Cayman Islands National Museum.** Built in 1833, FAMILY the historically significant clapboard home of the national museum has had several different incarnations over the years, serving as courthouse, jail, post office, and dance hall. It features an ongoing archaeological excavation of the Old Gaol and excellent 3-D bathymetric displays, murals, dioramas, and videos that illustrate local geology, flora and fauna, and island history. The first floor focuses on natural

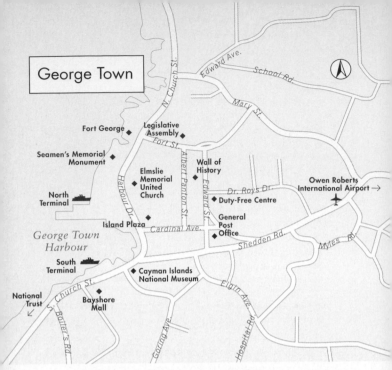

history, including a microcosm of Cayman ecosystems, from beaches to dry woodlands and swamps, and offers such interactive elements as a simulated sub. Upstairs, the cultural exhibit features renovated murals, video history reenactments, and 3-D back panels in display cases holding thousands of artifacts ranging from a 14-foot catboat with animatronic captain to old coins and rare documents painting a portrait of daily life and past industries such as shipbuilding and turtling, stressing Caymanians' resilience when they had little contact with the outside world. There are also temporary exhibits focusing on aspects of Caymanian culture, a local art collection, and interactive displays for kids. ⊠ *Harbour Dr., George Town, Grand Cayman* ☎ *345/949–8368* ⊕ *www.museum.ky* ⊠ *$8, $5.60 Sat.* ⊙ *Weekdays 9–5, Sat. 10–2.*

NEED A BREAK? Full of Beans Cafe. On the surprisingly large, eclectic, Asian-tinged menu using ultrafresh ingredients, standouts include homemade carrot cake, mango smoothies, cranberry-Brie-pecan salad, and rosemary-roasted portobello and pesto chicken paninis. Their espresso martini will perk up anyone

CLOSE UP

Maritime Heritage Trail

The National Trust for the Cayman Islands, National Museum, National Archive, Sister Islands Nature Tourism Project, and Department of the Environment have collaborated on a series of land-based sightseeing trails on Grand Cayman and the Sister Islands that commemorate the country's maritime heritage. Shoreside signs around the islands denote points of access and explain their historic or natural significance, from shipwreck sites to shorebird-sighting spots, chandlers' warehouses to lighthouses.

Brochures and posters are available at the National Trust and tourism offices on each island, as well as at many hotels. They provide additional information on turtling, shipbuilding, salvaging, fishing, and other sea-based economies. The project provides visitors with interactive edu-tainment as they explore the islands.

---

wanting a pick-me-up. Owner Cindy Butler fashions a feast for weary eyes as well, with rotating artworks (many for sale) and stylish mosaic mirrors contrasting with faux-brick walls and vintage hardwood tables. ⊠ *Pasadora Pl., Smith Rd., George Town, Grand Cayman* ☎ *345/943–2326, 345/814–0157*.

National Trust. For a wonderful map of the historic and natural attractions, go to the office of the National Trust. The Trust sells books and guides to Cayman. The fabulous website has more than 50 information sheets on cultural and natural topics from iguanas to schoolhouses. Take advantage of the regularly scheduled activities, from boat tours through the forests of the Central Mangrove Wetlands to cooking classes with local chefs to morning walking tours of historic George Town. Stop here first before you tour the island. Be forewarned: though the office is walkable from George Town, it's an often-hot 20-minute hike from downtown. ⊠ *Dart Park, 558 S. Church St., George Town, Grand Cayman* ☎ *345/749–1121* ⊕ *www.nationaltrust.org. ky* ☉ *Weekdays 9–5*.

SEVEN MILE BEACH

FAMILY **Camana Bay Observation Tower.** This 75-foot structure provides striking 360-degree panoramas of otherwise flat Grand Cayman, sweeping from George Town and Seven Mile Beach to the North Sound. The double-helix staircase

A traditional Cayman cottage at Boatswain's Beach

is impressive in its own right. Running alongside the steps (though an elevator is also available), a floor-to-ceiling mosaic replicates the look and feel of a dive from seabed to surface. Constructed of countless tiles in 114 different colors, it's one of the world's largest marine-themed mosaic installations. Benches and lookout points encourage you to take your time and take in the views as you ascend. Afterward you can enjoy 500-acre Camana Bay's gardens, waterfront boardwalk, and pedestrian paths lined with shops and restaurants, or frequent live entertainment. ⊠ *Extending between Seven Mile Beach and North Sound, 2 mi (3 km) north of George Town, Camana Bay, Grand Cayman* ☎ *345/640–3500* ⊕ *www.camanabay.com* ☜ *Free* ⊙ *Daily sunrise–10 pm.*

★ Fodor'sChoice **National Gallery.** A worthy nonprofit organization, this museum displays and promotes the range of Caymanian artists and craftspeople, both established and grassroots. The gallery coordinates a wealth of first-rate outreach programs for everyone from infants to inmates. It usually mounts six major exhibitions a year, including three large-scale retrospectives or thematic shows and multimedia installations. Director Natalie Urquhart also brings in international shows that somehow relate to the island, often inviting local artists for stimulating dialogue. The gallery hosts public slide shows, a lunchtime lecture series running in conjunction with current exhibits, Art

Flix (video presentations on art history, introduced with a short lecture and followed by a discussion led by curators or artists), and a CineClub (movie night). The gallery has also developed an Artist Trail Map with the Department of Tourism and can facilitate studio tours. There's an excellent shop and, new in 2014, an Art Cafe. ⊠ *Esterly Tibbetts Hwy. at Harquail Bypass, Seven Mile Beach, Grand Cayman* ☎ *345/945–8111* ⊕ *www.nationalgallery.org.ky* ☎ *Free* ⊘ *Weekdays 10–5, Sat. 10–3.*

2

WEST BAY

Cayman Motor Museum. This unexpected collection documents the magnificent obsession of one man, Norwegian magnate Andreas Ugland. More than 80 vehicles, preening like supermodels, gleam in ranks. "Holy hot-rod, Batman," it's one of the three original Batmobiles from the 1960's TV series. There's the world's first produced auto, an 1886 Benz! Tiers of classic Ferraris, Jags, Corvettes, BMWs, and more date back nearly a century, including such unique collectibles as Elton John's Bentley, the 1930 Phantom driven in the film *Yellow Rolls Royce*, and Queen Elizabeth II's first limo. You can go hog wild over Harleys and other bad-ass bikes. And well, just because, coffee grinders. This isn't actually mere kitchen kitsch: Peugeot started producing mills and grinders in the mid-19th century. An avid sailor, Mr. Ugland wants to start a boat museum as well. That might be fun but it likely won't capture the unlikely charm of this Cayman oddity. ⊠ *864 Northwest Point Rd., West Bay, Grand Cayman* ☎ *345/947–7741* ⊕ *www.caymanmotormuseum.com* ☎ *$15* ⊘ *Mon.–Sat. 9–5* ⊘ *Closed Sun.*

FAMILY **Cayman Turtle Farm.** Cayman's premier attraction, the Turtle Farm, has been transformed into a marine theme park. The expanded complex now has several souvenir shops and restaurants. Still, the turtles remain a central attraction, and you can tour ponds in the original research–breeding facility with thousands in various stages of growth, some up to 600 pounds and more than 70 years old. Turtles can be picked up from the tanks, a real treat for children and adults as the little creatures flap their fins and splash the water. Four areas—three aquatic and one dry—cover 23 acres; different-color bracelets determine access (the steep full-pass admission includes snorkeling gear). The park helps promote conservation, encouraging interaction (a tidal pool houses invertebrates such as starfish and crabs) and observation. Animal Program events include Keeper

CLOSE UP

Camana Bay

Dubbed a "new town" (in all senses of the term), ambitious in scope and philosophy, the mixed-use, master-planned Camana Bay stretches along 500 acres from Seven Mile Beach to the North Sound. It's a sustainable, traditional, and colorfully Caribbean—yet technologically cutting-edge—design, and ecologically sensitive to boot. Specifically designed by more than 100 consultants from several leading local and global firms as a gathering center to live, work, and play, Camana Bay has been carefully developed in three phases (the final phase is expected to be completed by 2017 and will include hotels and a marina, alongside residential and office development).

The four residential-office-retail courtyards feature unique feels and color schemes unifying native flora with surrounding walls, walks, and mosaics.

Streets were aligned to mitigate heat and to capture breezes. Plants were carefully chosen to attract birds and butterflies, and the development has green space galore, including artificial islands and harbors, as well as water features like canals and fountains.

The pedestrianized main street, called the Paseo, is lined with mostly high-end shops that are open late, restaurants, and entertainment (including a weekly farmers' market and a movie theater complex). The Paseo culminates in the Crescent, a waterfront plaza with restaurants, more gardens, interactive fountains, an esplanade, amphitheater, and public venues for fireworks to festivals. There are also jogging/biking trails, pocket parks, open spaces, and a beach. Residents and visitors are encouraged to park their cars and stroll (enhancing the green lifestyle) or just hang out.

Talks, where you might feed birds or iguanas, and biologists speaking about conservation and their importance to the ecosystem. The freshwater **Breaker's Lagoon,** replete with cascades plunging over moss-carpeted rocks evoking Cayman Brac, is the islands' largest pool. The saltwater **Boatswain's Lagoon,** replicating all the Cayman Islands and the Trench, teems with 14,000 denizens of the deep milling about a cannily designed synthetic reef. You can snorkel here (lessons and guided tours are available). Both lagoons have underwater 4-inch-thick acrylic panels that look directly into **Predator Reef,** home to six brown sharks, four nurse sharks, and other predatory fish such as tarpons, eels, and jacks. These predators can also be viewed from terra (or terror, as one guide jokes) firma. Make sure you check out feeding times! The free-flight **Aviary**, designed by consultants from Disney's Animal Kingdom, is a riot of color and noise as feathered friends represent the entire Caribbean basin, doubling as a rehabilitation center for Cayman Wildlife and Rescue. A winding interpretive **nature trail** culminates in the Blue Hole, a collapsed cave once filled with water. Audio tours are available with different focuses, from butterflies to bush medicine. The last stop is the living museum, **Cayman Street**, complete with facades duplicating different types of vernacular architecture; an herb and fruit garden; porch-side artisans, musicians, and storytellers; model catboats; live cooking on an old-fashioned caboose (outside kitchen) oven; and interactive craft demonstrations from painting mahogany to thatch weaving. ✉ *825 Northwest Point Rd., Box 812, West Bay, Grand Cayman* ☎ *345/949–3894* ⊕ *www.turtle.ky, www.boatswainsbeach. ky* ✍ *Comprehensive ticket $45 ($25 children under 12); Turtle Farm only, $30* ⊙ *Mon.–Sat. 8–4:30, Sun. 10–4. Lagoons close ½ hr to 2 hrs earlier.*

FAMILY **Dolphin Discovery.** If you ever dreamed of frolicking with Flipper, here's your (photo) opportunity, as the organizers of this global business promise a "touching experience." The well-maintained facility, certified by the Alliance of Marine Mammal Parks and Aquariums, offers three main options, essentially depending on time spent splashing in the enormous pool with the dolphins and stingrays. They range in price from $99 to $169 (kids receive a discount but must swim with an adult). The premium is the Royal Swim, which includes a dorsal tow and foot push, showcasing the amazing strength, speed, and agility of these majestic marine mammals. Other options offer a handshake, kiss, even a belly ride. All participants receive free entrance to their choice of Stingray City or the Turtle Farm across the street, taking some of the sting out of the high prices. ✉ *Northwest Point Rd., West Bay, Grand Cayman* ☎ *345/769–7946, 866/393–5158 toll-free from U.S., 345/949–7946* ⊕ *www. dolphindiscovery.com/grand-cayman.*

Hell. Quite literally the tourist trap from Hell, especially when overrun by cruise-ship passengers, this attraction does offer free admission, fun photo ops, and sublime surrealism. Its name refers to the quarter-acre of menacing shards of charred brimstone thrusting up like vengeful spirits (actually blackened and "sculpted" by acid-secreting algae and fungi over millennia). The eerie lunarscape is now cordoned off, but you can prove you had a helluva time by taking a photo from the observation deck. The attractions are the small post office and a gift shop where you can get cards and letters postmarked from Hell, not to mention wonderfully silly postcards titled "When Hell Freezes Over" (depicting bathing beauties on the beach), "The Devil Made Me Do It" bumper stickers, Scotch bonnet–based Hell sauce, and "The coolest shop in Hell" T-shirts. Ivan Farrington, the owner of the Devil's Hang-Out store, cavorts in a devil's costume (horn, cape, and tails), regaling you with demonically bad jokes. ⊠ *Hell Rd., West Bay, Grand Cayman* ☎ *345/949–3358* ⚏ *Free* ⊙ *Daily 9–6.*

EAST END AND NORTH SIDE

The Tourism Attraction Board and 14 leading eastern-district businesses (from Ocean Frontiers dive shop to Kaibo Beach Bar) and attractions developed the **"Discover the East" Adventure Card** to encourage visitors (and locals) to experience the beauty, culture, and heritage of Grand Cayman's eastern districts. The $16 card provides free admission to the Queen Elizabeth II Botanic Park and to Pedro St. James (normally $10 each), as well as gifts and discounts throughout Bodden Town, Cayman Kai, North Side, and the East End, from free desserts with dinner to $20 off diving.

FAMILY **Blowholes.** When the easterly trade winds blow hard, crashing waves force water into caverns and send impressive geysers shooting up as much as 20 feet through the ironshore. The blowholes were partially filled during Hurricane Ivan in 2004, so the water must be rough to recapture their former elemental drama. ⊠ *Frank Sound Rd., roughly 10 mi (16 km) east of Bodden Town, near East End, Grand Cayman.*

Bodden Town. In the island's original south-shore capital you can find an old cemetery on the shore side of the road. There are also the ruins of a fort and a wall erected by slaves in the 19th century. The National Trust runs tours of the restored 1840s Mission House. A curio shop serves as the entrance to what's called the Pirate's Caves ($8), partially underground natural formations that are more hokey (decked out with fake treasure chests and mannequins in pirate garb, with an outdoor petting zoo) than spooky. ⊠ *Grand Cayman.*

Cayman Islands Brewery. This brewery occupies the former Stingray facility; free tours are available on the hour

DID YOU KNOW?

The blowholes on Grand Cayman's south shore were formed when waves pushed seawater through the ceilings of caves under the ironshore, sending the spray up into the air.

CLOSE UP

Cayman House and Garden

The few original Caymanian cottages that exist represent a unique architectural vernacular cannily adapted to the climate and available resources. Foundation posts and floors were constructed from durable, termite-resistant ironwood. Wattle-and-daub walls were fashioned from basket-woven sticks plastered on both sides with lime daub (extracted coral burned with various woods). The earliest roofs were thatched with woven palm fronds (later shingled or topped with corrugated zinc); their peaks helped cool houses, as hot air rises. The kitchen was separate, usu-

ally just a "caboose" stove for cooking.

The other unusual custom, "backing sand," originated as a Christmas tradition, then became a year-round decorative statement. Women and children would tote woven-thatch baskets by moonlight to the beach, bringing "back" glittering white sand to cover their front yards. They'd rake intricate patterns and adorn the sand with sinuous conch-shell paths. The yard was also swept Saturday so it would look well tended after Sunday services. A side benefit was that it helped reduce insect infestation.

(weekdays from 9 to 4 by appointment only). The guide will explain the iconic imagery of the bottle and label, and the nearly three-week process: 7 days' fermentation, 10 days' lagering (storage), and 1 day in the bottling tank. The brewery's ecofriendly features are also championed: local farmers receive the spent grains used to produce the beer to serve as cattle feed at no charge, while waste liquid is channeled into one of the Caribbean's most advanced water-treatment systems. Then enjoy your complimentary tasting with the knowledge that you're helping the local environment and economy. ⊠ 366 Shamrock Rd., Red Bay, Grand Cayman ☎ 345/947–6699 ⊕ www.cib.ky ☜ Free ⊙ Weekdays 9–5.

Mission House. The Mission House is a classic gabled two-story Caymanian home on wooden posts, with wattle-and-daub accents, dating to the 1840s and restored by the National Trust. The building earned its sobriquet thanks to early missionaries, teachers, and families who lived here while helping establish the Presbyterian ministry and school in Bodden Town. Shards of 19th-century glass and ceramics found on-site and period furnishings are on display. The posted opening hours are irregular, especially during the off-season. ✉ *63 Gun Square Rd., Bodden Town, Grand Cayman* ☎ *345/749–1132* ⊕ *www.nationaltrust.org.ky* ✉ *$7* ☉ *Weekdays 9–1; last tour at noon.*

★ Fodor'sChoice **Pedro St. James Castle.** Built in 1780, the great-house is Cayman's oldest stone structure and the only remaining late-18th-century residence on the island. In its capacity as courthouse and jail, it was the birthplace of Caymanian democracy, where in December 1831 the first elected parliament was organized and in 1835 the Slavery Abolition Act signed. The structure still has original or historically accurate replicas of sweeping verandahs, mahogany floors, rough-hewn wide-beam ceilings, outside louvers, stone and oxblood- or mustard-color lime-wash-painted walls, brass fixtures, and Georgian furnishings (from tea caddies to canopy beds to commodes). Paying obsessive attention to detail, the curators even fill glasses with faux wine. The mini-museum also includes a hodge-podge of displays from slave emancipation to old stamps. The buildings are surrounded by 8 acres of natural parks and woodlands. You can stroll through landscaping of native Caymanian flora and experience one of the most spectacular views on the island from atop the dramatic Great Pedro Bluff. First watch the impressive multimedia theater show, complete with smoking pots, misting rains, and two film screens where the story of Pedro's Castle is presented on the hour. The poignant Hurricane Ivan Memorial outside uses text, images, and symbols to represent important aspects of that horrific 2004 natural disaster. ✉ *Pedro Castle Rd., Savannah, Grand Cayman* ☎ *345/947–3329* ⊕ *www.pedrostjames.ky* ✉ *$10* ☉ *Daily 9–5.*

Pirate's Caves. You enter the Pirate's Caves through a surprisingly good curio shop (the owner is noted for jewelry fashioned from doubloons). Outside, ceramic "skulls" embedded into banyan trees and mini gravestones enhance the supposed spookiness. Younger kids should adore the playground and mini zoo with freshwater Brazilian stingrays, turtles, parrots, macaws, iguanas, agoutis (a large rodent), mountain goats, and farm animals like chickens, the pig Percy, and the horse Spirit. The caves themselves are pure yo-ho-hokum, tricked up with more faux "skeletons," swords jutting from limestone formations, and other rusted artifacts of dubious authenticity (such as fake treasure chests), lanterns, and conch shells, as well as an authentic fossilized bone or two. Beware the steep descent (with only rope handrails). Very informative sheets on history and the native plants are provided, as well as good interpretive signage within the grounds. ⊠ *South Shore Rd., Bodden Town, Grand Cayman* ☎ *345/947–3122* ☎ *$8* ⊙ *Daily 9–6.*

★ **Fodor's** Choice **Queen Elizabeth II Botanic Park.** This 65-acre wilderness preserve showcases a wide range of indigenous and nonindigenous tropical vegetation, approximately 2,000 species in total. Splendid sections include numerous water features from limpid lily ponds to cascades; a Heritage Garden with a traditional cottage and "caboose" (outside kitchen) that includes crops that might have been planted on Cayman a century ago; and a Floral Colour Garden arranged by color, the walkway wandering through sections of pink, red, orange, yellow, white, blue, mauve, lavender, and purple. A 2-acre lake and adjacent wetlands includes three islets that provide a habitat and breeding ground for native birds just as showy as the floral displays: green herons, black-necked stilts, American coots, blue-winged teal, cattle egrets, and rare West Indian whistling ducks. The nearly mile-long Woodland Trail encompasses every Cayman ecosystem from wetland to cactus thicket, buttonwood swamp to lofty woodland with imposing mahogany trees. You'll encounter birds, lizards, turtles, agoutis, and more, but the park's star residents are the protected endemic blue iguanas, found only in Grand Cayman. The world's most endangered iguana, they're the focus of the National Trust's Blue Iguana Recovery Program, a captive breeding and reintroduction facility. This section of the park is usually closed to the general public, though released "blue dragons" hang out in the vicinity. The Trust conducts 90-minute behind-the-scenes safaris Monday–Saturday at 11 am for $30. ⊠ *367 Botanic Rd., East End, Grand Cayman* ☎ *345/947–9462* ⊕ *www.botanic-park.ky* ☎ *$10; ages 12 and under free with parent* ⊙ *Daily 9–5:30; last admission 1 hr before closing.*

Wreck of the Ten Sails Park. This lonely, lovely park on Grand Cayman's windswept eastern tip commemorates the island's most (in)famous shipwreck. On February 8, 1794, the *Cordelia,* heading a convoy of 58 square-rigged merchant vessels en route from Jamaica to England, foundered on one of the treacherous East End reefs. Its warning cannon fire was tragically misconstrued as a call to band more closely together due to imminent pirate attack, and nine more ships ran aground. The local sailors, who knew those rough seas, demonstrated great bravery in rescuing all 400-odd seamen. Popular legend claims (romantically but inaccurately) that

King George III granted the islands an eternal tax exemption. Queen Elizabeth II dedicated the park's plaque in 1994. Interpretive signs document the historic details. The ironically peaceful headland provides magnificent views of the reef (including more recent shipwrecks); bird-watching is superb from here half a mile south along the coast to the Lighthouse Park, perched on a craggy bluff. ⊠ *Gun Bay, East End, Grand Cayman* ☎ *345/949–0121 (National Trust)* ⊉ *Free* ⊗ *Daily*.

SHOPPING

On Grand Cayman the good news is that there's no sales tax *and* plenty of duty-free merchandise including jewelry, china, crystal, perfumes, and cameras. Savings on luxury goods, though rarely as great as good sales in big cities or at outlet malls in the United States, range between 10% and 25%. Notable exceptions are liquor, which is available minus that tariff only at specially designated shops, and haute couture (though the ritzier resort shops stock some designer labels). "Brand Cayman" is the local nickname for the glamorous shops along Cardinal Avenue, the local answer to New York's Madison Avenue and Beverly Hills's Rodeo Drive. Esteemed names include Cartier, Waterford, and Wedgwood.

Worthy local items include woven thatch mats and baskets, jewelry made from a marblelike stone called Caymanite (from Cayman Brac's cliffs, a striated amalgam of several metals), and authentic sunken treasure often fashioned into jewelry, though the last is never cheap (request a certificate of authenticity if one isn't offered). You'll also find individual artists' ateliers and small, colorful craft shops whose owners often love discussing the old days and traditions. Bear in mind that most major attractions feature extensive and/or intriguing gift shops, whether the Turtle Farm or the National Gallery.

Local palate pleasers include treats made by the Tortuga Rum Company (both the famed cakes and the actual distilled spirit, including a sublime 12-year-old rum), Cayman Honey, Cayman Taffy, and Cayman Sea Salt (from the ecofriendly "farm" of the same name). Seven Fathoms is the first working distillery actually in Cayman itself, its award-winning rums aged underwater (hence the name). Also seek out such gastronomic goodies as jams, sauces, and vinegars from Hawley Haven and Whistling Duck

Blue Dragons

CLOSE UP

Co-sponsored by the Botanic Park and the National Trust, the **Blue Iguana Recovery Program** (⊕ www.blueiguana.ky) is a model captive breeding plan for the remarkable reptiles that only two decades ago faced total extinction. The Grand Cayman blue iguana lived on the island for millennia until man arrived, its only natural predator the racer snake. Until recently they were the world's most critically endangered species, functionally extinct with only 25 remaining in the wild. BIRP has released more than 200 into the Salina Reserve, with an ultimate repopulation goal of 1,000 if they can breed successfully in the wild.

The National Trust conducts safaris six mornings a week, giving you a chance to see hatchlings in the cages, camouflaged toddlers, and breeding-age adults like Mad Max and Blue Blue. Most of the iguanas raised here are released at two years by the Wildlife Conservation Society with a microchip implant tag for radio tracking and color-coded beading ("their navel rings," jokes a guide) for unique identification. Tones fluctuate according to light-ing and season, brightening to azure during the April–May breeding period. Guides explain the gestation and incubation periods and the pairing of potential mates ("some are too dominant, and we don't want inbreeding like Appalachian hillbillies, leading to potential mutations or sterility").

If you can't make it to the park, look for the 15 larger-than-life, one-of-a-kind outdoor sculptures commissioned from local artists scattered around the island. You can download maps of the Blue Dragon Trail from the BIRP, National Trust, and Botanic Park sites. Many hotels also stock leaflets with maps and fun facts (the iguanas live up to 70 years, grow to 6 feet in length, and weigh 25 pounds). You can even purchase custom blue iguana products (helping fund research), such as Joel Friesch's limited-edition hand-painted bobbleheads (blues bob their heads rapidly as a territorial warning) packaged in a bright yellow hard cardboard box. You can also volunteer for a working vacation (or longer field-work study stint) online.

Farms on the eastern half of the island. Cigar lovers, take note: Some shops carry famed Cuban brands, but you must enjoy them on the island; bringing them back to the United States is illegal.

An almost unbroken line of strip malls runs from George Town through Seven Mile Beach, most of them presenting shopping and dining options galore. The ongoing Camana Bay mega-development already glitters with glam shops, including Island Companies' largest and grandest store offering the hautest name-brand jewelry, watches, and duty-free goods.

GEORGE TOWN

SHOPPING CENTERS

Bayshore Mall. Optimally located downtown and one of the leading shopaholics' targets (you can't miss the cotton-candy colors), this mall contains a Kirk Freeport department-store branch (Tag Heuer to Herend porcelain, Mikimoto to Mont Blanc), swank Lalique and Lladró boutiques, La Parfumerie (which often offers makeovers and carries 450 beauty brands), and other usual luxury culprits. ✉ *S. Church St., George Town, Grand Cayman.*

Cayside Courtyard. This small courtyard shopping center is noted for its specialty jewelers and antiques dealers. ✉ *Harbour Dr., George Town, Grand Cayman.*

Duty Free Plaza. This mall caters to more casual shoppers with the T-shirt Factory, Island Treasures, Havana Cigars, Blackbeard's Rumcake Bakery, and the Surf Shop. It also contains a kid-pleasing 12,000-gallon saltwater aquarium with sharks, eels, and stingrays. ✉ *S. Church St., George Town, Grand Cayman.*

Island Plaza. Here you'll find 15 duty- and tax-free stores, including Swarovski Boutique, Island Jewellers, and Churchill's Cigars (with bars like Margaritaville to destress in after binge shopping). ✉ *Harbour Dr., George Town, Grand Cayman.*

Kirk Freeport Plaza. This downtown shopping center, home to the Kirk Freeport flagship department store, is ground zero for couture; it's also known for its boutiques selling fine watches and jewelry, china, crystal, leather, perfumes, and cosmetics, from Baccarat to Bulgari, Raymond Weil to Waterford and Wedgwood (the last two share their own autonomous boutique). Just keep walking—there's plenty of eye-catching, mind-boggling consumerism in all directions: Boucheron, Cartier (with its own mini-boutique), Chanel, Clinique, Christian Dior, Clarins, Estée Lauder, Fendi, Guerlain, Lancôme, Yves Saint Laurent, Issey Miyake, Jean

Words and Music

Local books and CDs make wonderful gifts and souvenirs. Recapture the flavor of your stay with *Miss Cleo's Cayman Kitchen*—subtitled "Treasured Recipes from the East End"—by Cleopatra Conolly, or *Cook' in Little Cayman,* by irrepressible Gladys Howard, a longtime resort owner who studied under James Beard and Julia Child. Plunge into *Diary of a Dirtbag Divemaster* by Little Cayman's Terry Thompson; it's a fact-inspired fiction recounting the escapades of six dive instructors working on a small Caribbean island. Another Little Cayman expat, Gay Morse, relates her own amusing behind-the-scenes anecdotes about teaching scuba and helping operate a small resort, *So You Want to Live on an Island?* H. George "Barefoot Man" Nowak's *Which Way to the Islands?* is another hilarious collection of only-in-the-Caribbean stories. Noted artist Nasaria Suckoo-Chollette pens poems and short stories based on local culture and folklore, including *Story Telling Rundown.* On a more serious note, celebrated photographer Courtney Platt documented the devastation wrought by Hurricane Ivan in the 330 striking images composing *Paradise Interrupted.*

Sway back home to soca, reggae, calypso, and Carib-country beats. Grand Cayman has several recording studios, including the state-of-the-art Hopscotch, whose Platinum label records both Lammie and MOJ. Garden Studios is owned by popular group Hi Tide. C and B Studio records exclusively for Sea and B—Earl la Pierre and Barefoot Man (the latter alone has 28 CDs and counting). Other worthwhile local recording artists include jazz masters Gary Ebanks and Intransit, hard rockers Ratskyn and Cloudburst, and sultry soulster Karen Edie.

Paul Gaultier, Nina Ricci, Rolex, Roberto Coin, Rosenthal and Royal Doulton china, and more. ✉ *Cardinall Ave., George Town, Grand Cayman.*

Landmark. Stores in the Landmark sell perfumes, treasure coins, and upscale beachwear; Breezes by the Bay restaurant is upstairs. ✉ *Harbour Dr., George Town, Grand Cayman.*

ART GALLERIES

The art scene has exploded in the past decade, moving away from typical Caribbean motifs and "primitive" styles. Cayman's most famous artist had been the late Gladwyn Bush, fondly known as Miss Lassie, who died in 2003. She began painting her intuitive religious subjects after a "vision" when she was 62. She also decorated the facade, interior walls, furnishings, even appliances of her home (which at this writing was converted into a museum and workshop space, at the junction of South Shore Road and Walkers Road). Bush was awarded the MBE (Most Excellent Order of the British Empire) in 1997, and her work is found in collections from Paris to Baltimore (whose American Visionary Art Museum owns several canvases). Bendel Hydes is another widely respected local (who moved to SoHo more than two decades ago yet still paints Caymanian-inspired works that capture the islands' elemental colors and dynamic movement). Leading expat artists include Joanne Sibley and Charles Long, both of whom create more figurative Cayman-theme art from luminous landscapes and shining portraits to pyrotechnically hued flora. Several artists' home-studios double as galleries, including the internationally known Al Ebanks, the controversial Luelan Bodden, and fanciful sculptor Horacio Esteban; the National Gallery has a list.

Al Ebanks Studio Gallery. This gallery shows the eponymous artist's versatile, always provocative work in various media. Since you're walking into his home as well as atelier, everything is on display. Clever movable panels maximize space "like Art Murphy beds." His work, while inspired by his home, could never be labeled traditional Caribbean art, exhibiting vigorous movement through abstract swirls of color and textural contrasts. Though nonrepresentational (save for his equally intriguing sculpture and ceramics), the focal subject from carnivals to iguanas is always subtly apparent. Ask him about the Native Sons art movement he cofounded. ⊠ *186B Shedden Rd., George Town, Grand Cayman* ☎ *345/927–5365, 345/949–0693.*

Artifacts. On the George Town waterfront, Artifacts sells Spanish pieces of eight, doubloons, and Halcyon Days enamels (hand-painted collectible pillboxes made in England), as well as antique maps and other collectibles. ⊠ *Cayside Courtyard, Harbour Dr., George Town, Grand Cayman* ☎ *345/949–2442* ⊕ *www.artifacts.com.ky.*

Cathy Church's Underwater Photo Centre and Gallery. Come see a collection of the acclaimed underwater shutterbug's spectacular color and limited-edition black-and-white underwater photos. Have Cathy autograph her latest coffee-table book and regale you with anecdotes of her globe-trotting adventures. The store also carries the latest marine camera

Going Native Sons

In 1995 three artists founded a collaborative called Native Sons, adding a fourth in 1996, and currently featuring 10 members. Their primary goal is to develop and promote Caymanian artists. Though they work in different mediums and styles, the group resists facile characterization and challenges conventions as to what characterizes "Caribbean" art. One of the core members, Al Ebanks, has achieved major international success, but he admits that the islands can be provincial: "Cayman doesn't always recognize talent unless you're signed to a gallery overseas."

Though the National Gallery and the Cayman National Cultural Foundation both vigorously support the movement and are committed to sponsoring local artists, some Native Sons members feel their agendas can be too safe, betraying the bureaucratic, corporate mentality they admit is often necessary to raise funds for nonprofit institutions. They have also felt subtle pressure to conform commercially and an inherent bias toward expat artists, whose work often depicts the literally sunnier side of Caymanian life, and resent what they perceived to be censorship of rawer, edgier works, including depictions of nudity in arch-conservative Cayman.

They have sought to push the boundaries for both institutions and private galleries. "Yes, art is art and shouldn't be grounded in national stereotypes, though my country inspires my work.... We just want balance," Ebanks says. "People look at more challenging work and ask 'Where's the boats?' We live that scene!"

Obviously this is a hot-button topic on a tiny island. Chris Christian, who originally achieved success through representational beach scenes but wanted to expand and experiment, uses the Cayman term "crabs in a bucket," describing how "artists in a small pool scratch and scramble over each other, succeeding by badmouthing others." Which is why the support structure and philosophy of Native Sons is so vital: They help each other negotiate "that constant balance between commercial success and artistic integrity."

Other members include cofounder Wray Banker, Randy Chollette, Nasaria Suckoo-Chollette, Gordon Solomon, Horacio Esteban, and Nickola McCoy. These native sons and daughters all passionately believe art isn't merely about pretty pictures and uncompromisingly believe in preserving Caymanian culture and freedom of expression.

equipment, and she'll schedule private underwater photography instruction as well on her own dive boat outfitted with special graphics-oriented computers to critique your work. She also does wedding photography, both above and underwater. If you don't have time to stop in, check out the world's largest underwater photo installation, 9 feet high and 145 feet long, at Grand Cayman's Owen Roberts Airport Baggage Claim area, curated by Cathy and her team. ⊠ *S. Church St., George Town, Grand Cayman* ☎ *345/949–7415* ⊕ *www.cathychurch.com.*

Guy Harvey's Gallery and Shoppe. This is where world-renowned marine biologist, conservationist, and artist Guy Harvey showcases his aquatic-inspired action-packed art in nearly every conceivable medium, branded tableware, and sportswear (even logo soccer balls and Zippos). The soaring, two-story 4,000-square-foot space is almost more theme park than store, with monitors playing his sportfishing videos, wood floors inlaid with tile duplicating rippling water, dangling catboats "attacked" by lifelike shark models, and life-size murals honoring such classics as Hemingway's *Old Man and the Sea.* Original paintings, sculpture, and drawings are expensive, but there's something (tile art, prints, lithographs, and photos) in most price ranges. ⊠ *49 S. Church St., George Town, Grand Cayman* ☎ *345/943–4891* ⊕ *www.guyharvey.com.*

Pure Art. About 1½ miles (2½ km) south of George Town, Pure Art purveys wit, warmth, and whimsy right from the wildly colored front steps. Its warren of rooms resembles a garage sale run amok or a quirky grandmother's attic spilling over with unexpected finds, from foodstuffs to functional and wearable art. ⊠ *S. Church St. at Denham-Thompson Way, George Town, Grand Cayman* ☎ *345/949–9133* ⊕ *www.pureart.ky.*

Seven Fathoms Rum. Surprisingly, this growing company, established in 2008, is Cayman's first distillery. It's already garnered medals in prestigious international competitions for its artisanal small-batch rums. You can stop by for a tasting and self-guided tour, learning how they age the rum at 7 fathoms (42 feet) deep; supposedly the natural kinetic motion of the currents enables the rum to maximize contact with the oak, extracting its rich flavors and enhancing complexity. Based on the results, it's not just yo-ho-hokum. ⊠ *65 Bronze Rd., George Town, Grand Cayman* ☎ *345/925–5379, 345/926–8186* ⊕ *www.sevenfathomsrum.com.*

DID YOU KNOW?

At popular Stingray Sandbar in Grand Cayman, the rays come right up to the excursion boats and will eat out of your hand.

Not Just a Guy Thing

Guy Harvey is a man of many hats. He has a PhD in marine biology and is also a world-class angler, renowned aquatic wildlife artist, cinematographer, TV producer, presenter of a weekly TV program titled *Portraits from the Deep,* clothing designer, and dedicated environmentalist.

Anyone passing through the Fort Lauderdale airport has seen his dramatic three-story mural (a smaller mural may once again adorn Grand Cayman's Owen Roberts Airport). His art features meticulous composition and vibrant color, capturing the adrenaline-pumping action. "I try to humanize them, give them character in my paintings," Harvey says, though hardly in dewy, Disney-esque fashion.

Growing up a 10th-generation Jamaican, he loved fishing and diving with his father from an early age. Obsessed by all things aquatic, Harvey first gained notice in art circles with a 1985 Kingston exhibit of pen-and-ink drawings based on Hemingway's *Old Man and the Sea,* a recurring theme: man and animal bonding and exhibiting grace under pressure in their struggle for survival.

He moved to Cayman during Jamaica's political upheaval in the late 1970s. He liked Cayman's similar culture and cuisine, British heritage, and proximity to both Jamaica and Florida. Harvey has used his high profile synergistically as an artist, angler, author, and documentarian to strike merchandising deals, creating apparel and housewares lines and restaurants, pouring many of the profits back into research. He still travels the world on interactive marine programs such as following tagged sharks from Belize to Brazil. These expeditions serve a dual purpose: "…saving the environment while inspiring me artistically."

Harvey has consistently supported "catch and release" ethics for game fish around the world. He works closely with many conservation organizations to help protect global fishery resources and was appointed a trustee of the International Game Fish Association in 1992; six years later he was voted the IGFA's first-ever "Lifetime Achievement Award" from the World Fishing Awards Committee. The nonprofit Guy Harvey Research Institute was established with the Oceanographic Center of Nova Southeastern University in 1999 to support effective conservation and restoration of fish resources and biodiversity. His views can be controversial. Commenting on dolphin swim programs, he has said: "Dolphin safety is one of the biggest lies foisted on the public."

CAMERAS

Camera Store. The Camera Store has friendly and knowledgeable service, lots of duty-free digital cameras, accessories, and fast photo printing from self-service kiosks. ✉ *32 Goring Ave., George Town, Grand Cayman* ☎ *345/949–8359* ⊕ *www.thecamerastorecayman.com.*

CIGARS

Churchill's Cigars. A cigar-store Indian points the way into this tobacco emporium, which sells the island's largest selection of authentic Cubanos (and other imports), including such names as Upmann, Romeo y Julieta, and Cohiba, almost fetishistically displayed in the dark, clubby surroundings. The enthusiastic staff will advise on drink pairings (bold older rum for a Montecristo No. 2, cognac for smaller Partagas Shorts, a single-malt Scotch such as Glenmorangie for the Bolivar Belicoso Fino). There's a small airport branch as well. ✉ *Island Plaza, Harbour Dr., George Town, Grand Cayman* ☎ *345/945–6141* ⊕ *www. islandcompaniesltd.com/stores/churchills-cigars.*

CLOTHING

Arabus. The store carries primarily classy, classic ready-to-wear and knockoffs—though not at rip-off prices—for both sexes, casual to dressy, in flowing silk and cushy cashmere (for back home). ✉ *West Wind Bldg., 8 Fort St., George Town, Grand Cayman* ☎ *345/949–4620.*

Blue Wave. Your adrenalin starts pumping as soon as you enter this so-called lifestyle wear-surf shop. All the accoutrements you need to play the Big Kahuna are handsomely displayed, from sandals to sunglasses, Billabong plaid shirts to Quicksilver shorts, surfboards to ecosensitive Olukai footwear (talk to the clerks and you're ready to sign up for Greenpeace). ✉ *10 Shedden Rd., George Town, Grand Cayman* ☎ *345/949–8166.*

FOODSTUFFS

There are seven modern, U.S.-style supermarkets (three of them have full-service pharmacies) on Grand Cayman. Ask for the one nearest you. The biggest difference you'll find between these and supermarkets on the mainland is the prices, which are about 25%–30% more than at home.

Foster's Food Fair-IGA. The island's biggest supermarket chain has five stores. The Airport Centre and Strand stores have full-service pharmacies. These stores are open from Monday through Saturday, 7 am to 11 pm. ✉ *Airport Centre, 63*

Dorcy Dr., George Town, Grand Cayman ☎ *345/949–5155, 345/945–3663* ⊕ *www.fosters-iga.com.*

Kirk Supermarket and Pharmacy. This store is open Monday through Thursday from 7 am to 10 pm (until 11 pm Friday and Saturday) and is a particularly good source for traditional Caymanian fast food (oxtail, curried goat) and beverages at the juice bar. It also carries the largest selection of organic and special dietary products; the pharmacy stocks various homeopathic and herbal remedies. ✉ *413 Eastern Ave. near intersection with West Bay Rd., George Town, Grand Cayman* ☎ *345/949–7022* ⊕ *www. kirksupermarket.ky.*

Tortuga Rum Company. This company bakes, then vacuum-seals, more than 10,000 of its world-famous rum cakes daily, adhering to the original "secret" century-old recipe. There are eight flavors, from banana to Blue Mountain coffee. The 12-year-old rum, blended from private stock though actually distilled in Guyana, is a connoisseur's delight for after-dinner sipping. You can buy a fresh rum cake at the airport on the way home at the same prices as at the factory store. ✉ *N. Sound Rd., Industrial Park, George Town, Grand Cayman* ☎ *345/943–7663* ⊕ *www. tortugarumcakes.com.*

JEWELRY

Although you can find black-coral products in Grand Cayman, they're controversial. Most of the coral sold here comes from Belize and Honduras; Cayman Islands marine law prohibits the removal of live coral from its own sea. Black coral grows at a glacial rate (3 inches per decade) and is an endangered species. Cayman, however, is famed for artisans working with the material; shops are recommended, but let your conscience dictate your purchases.

Balaclava Jewellers. This shop is the domain of Martina and Philip Cadien, who studied at Germany's prestigious Pforzheim Goldsmithing School. The showroom sparkles appropriately, with breathtaking handcrafted pieces—usually naturally colored diamonds set in platinum or 18K white, yellow, and rose gold—framed and lovingly, almost sensuously lighted. Although there are simpler strands, this is a place where flash holds sway; the prices take your breath away, but the gems are flawless. ✉ *Governors Sq., West Bay Rd., Seven Mile Beach, Grand Cayman* ☎ *345/945–5788* ⊕ *www.balaclava-jewellers.com.*

CLOSE UP

Cayman Craft Market ✗

This open-air marketplace run by the Tourism Attraction Board at Hog Sty Bay, smack in the middle of George Town, is artists' central, helping maintain old-time Caymanian skills. The vendors offer locally made leather, thatch, wood, and shell items. You'll also find dolls, hats, carved parrots, bead and seed jewelry, hand-painted thatch bags and bonnets, and hand-carved waurie (also spelled warri) boards—an ancient African game using seeds (or the more modern marbles).

Also available here are Sea Salt (and their luxury bath product);

Hawley Haven Farm products (Mrs. Laurie Hawley's delectable papaya, tamarind, and guava jams; spicy mango chutney; thyme vinegar; Cayman honey; and jerk sauce; as well as her painted folkloric characters on handmade sun-dried paper made with native flowers, leaves, and herbs); the Cayman Tropicals line of fragrant fruit-based hair and skin-care products; and North Side's Whistling Duck Farm specialties from soursop to sea grape jams and jellies. Every month highlights a different area of the Cayman Islands, from Cayman Brac to Bodden Town.

Island Time. Locals appreciate Island Time for its affordable line of watches, especially top-notch Swiss brands, from Movado to Marvin to Maurice Lacroix. There's another branch with similar inventory in the Flagship Building. ✉ *Island Plaza, Cardinal Ave., George Town, Grand Cayman* ☎ *345/946–2333* ⊕ *www.islandcompaniesltd.com/ stores/island-time.*

Magnum Jewelers. Befitting its name, Magnum Jewelers traffics in high-caliber pieces by the elite likes of Girard-Perregaux and Harry Winston for a high-powered clientele. President Harry Chandi travels the world, his keen eye sourcing distinctive contemporary watches and bijoux (especially increasingly rare colored diamonds) for his equally glittery celebrity clientele, who also appreciate a bargain like the rest of us. Smaller spenders might appreciate the whimsical items such as pendants with hand-painted enamel sandals or crystal-encrusted purses. ✉ *Cardinal Plaza, Cardinal Ave., George Town, Grand Cayman* ☎ *345/946–9199* ⊕ *www.magnumjewelers.com.*

SEVEN MILE BEACH

SHOPPING CENTERS

Galleria Plaza. Nicknamed Blue Plaza for its azure hue, Galleria Plaza features several galleries and exotic home-accessories stores dealing in Oriental rugs or Indonesian furnishings, as well as more moderate souvenir shops hawking T-shirts and swimwear. ⊠ *West Bay Rd., Seven Mile Beach, Grand Cayman.*

The Strand Shopping Centre. This mall has branches of Tortuga Rum and Blackbeard's Liquor, and banks galore—the better to withdraw cash for shops with cachet like Polo Ralph Lauren and another Kirk Freeport (this branch particularly noteworthy for china and crystal, from Kosta Boda to Baccarat, as well as a second La Parfumerie). ⊠ *West Bay Rd., Seven Mile Beach, Grand Cayman.*

West Shore Shopping Centre. Dubbed Pink Plaza for reasons that become obvious upon approach, West Shore offers upscale boutiques and galleries (tenants range from Sotheby's International Realty to the Body Shop). ⊠ *West Bay Rd., Seven Mile Beach, Grand Cayman.*

ART GALLERIES

Ritz-Carlton Gallery. This gallery more than fulfilled one of the resort's conditions upon securing rights to build, which was to commission local arts and artisans to help decorate the public spaces. The corridor-cum-bridge spanning West Bay Road became a gallery where Chris Christian of Cayman Traditional Arts curates quarterly exhibitions of Cayman's finest (there are also themed shows devoted to photography and local kids' art). Each piece is for sale; CTA or the hotel will mediate in the negotiations between artist and buyer at a favorable commission. ⊠ *Ritz-Carlton Grand Cayman, West Bay Rd., Seven Mile Beach, Grand Cayman* ☎ *345/943–9000.*

BOOKS

Books & Books. The Miami independent bookseller opertes this outlet in Grand Cayman. Regular events include author readings and "Floetry," when poets and performers express themselves at the open mike. An entire room is devoted to kids with toys, educational games, and books from toddler to YA. ⊠ *45 Market St., Camana Bay, Grand Cayman* ☎ *345/640–2665.*

CIGARS

Havana Club Cigars. This store is the brainchild of Raglan Roper, who sailed from Florida to Cayman a quarter decade ago, stopping in Cuba en route. Immediately hooked on the cigars, cuisine, and culture, he eventually opened a Cayman shop, then expanded (he also owns a Cuban restaurant). In addition to the famed brands, the attraction is the irresistible in-house *torcedor* (cigar roller), Jesus Lara Perez, who rotates demonstrations between the stores. Jesus started working at 14 in the Cuban cigar factory La Isolina in Santa Clara, eventually becoming chief cigar roller for other leading brands. ✉ *West Shore Center, 508 West Bay Rd., Seven Mile Beach, Grand Cayman* ☎ *345/946–0523* ⊕ *www.havanaclub-cigars.com.*

FOODSTUFFS

FAMILY **Cayman Taffy.** Visitors to this genial candy store can satisfy their curiosity along with their taste buds by viewing the candy-making process in restored vintage equipment dating back to the early 20th century. Then sample saltwater taffy, caramel corn, and brittle in such exotic flavors as banana, coconut, mango, passion fruit, and Jamaican rum. The packaging, in coconut shells or boldly painted boxes, is almost as delectable. ✉ *West Shore Center, West Bay Rd., Seven Mile Beach, Grand Cayman* ☎ *345/943–2333* ⊕ *www.caymantaffy.net.*

JEWELRY

24K-Mon Jewelers. This store sells works of art from many jewelers, including Wyland, Merry-Lee Rae, and Stephen Douglas, as well as designs courtesy of owner-goldsmith Gale Tibbetts and her friends, incorporating everything from Swarovski crystals to Spanish doubloons. Most pieces are inspired by the sea. The adjacent gallery is one of the few commercial outlets for local artists such as Miguel Powery. ✉ *Buckingham Sq., Seven Mile Beach, Grand Cayman* ☎ *345/949–1499* ⊕ *www.24k-mon.com.*

Mitzi's Fine Jewelry. Mitzi's is a treasure trove of salvaged 18th-century coins, silver, Caymanite pieces, and black coral; the store also carries Italian porcelain and the Carrera y Carrera line of jewelry and sculptures. Self-taught, vivacious proprietor Mitzi Callan, who specializes in handmade pieces, is usually on hand to help. She also heads the Starvin' Artists co-op and also opened an intriguing local organic cosmetics/toiletries store next door. ✉ *5 Bay*

Harbour Centre, West Bay Rd., Seven Mile Beach, Grand Cayman ☎ *345/945–5014.*

WEST BAY

HANDICRAFTS AND SOUVENIRS

Bed Buddies. The name of this store refers to husband-wife team Bonnie and Fernando Thompson, who fashion lovely jewelry, bags, and baubles from local materials, including whelk shells, coconut husks, tree resin, and distinctive seeds from cat's claw to Cayman red apple. ⊠ *Hell Rd., West Bay, Grand Cayman* ☎ *345/917–1182, 345/929–8017* ⊕ *www.bedbuddiescreation.com.*

EAST END AND NORTH SIDE

ART GALLERIES

Bodden Town Art Shop. This shop purveys a grab bag of goodies, from homemade jellies to giclee prints, woven thatch handbags to hardwood and bronze sculpture. Top local and expat artists such as Randy Chollette and Avril Ward also exhibit here. ⊠ *293 Bodden Town Rd., next to Pirate Caves, Bodden Town, Grand Cayman* ☎ *345/943–2827.*

NasArt. At the home-studio of Luelan Bodden, virtually every surface is painted with wild images and hues. One of Cayman's most exciting, controversial artists, he works in various media and is deliberately provocative with a sociopolitical slant. ⊠ *Crewe Rd., Red Bay, Grand Cayman* ☎ *345/945–8278.*

FOODSTUFFS

Hurley's Marketplace. Hurley's is open Monday through Saturday from 7 am to 11 pm. ⊠ *Grand Harbour Shopping Centre, 1053 Crewe Rd., Red Bay, Grand Cayman* ☎ *345/947–8488* ⊕ *www.hurleys.ky.*

WHERE TO EAT IN GRAND CAYMAN

By Jordan
Simon

No indigenous peoples or gaggle of contentious colonial powers left much of an imprint on Grand Cayman cuisine, as was the case on many other islands. Until recently, the strongest culinary contributions to Cayman cuisine came from nearby Jamaica and, to a lesser extent, Cuba, though the worst of the British pub tradition lingered in pasties and heavy puddings. Fortunately, since the boom of the late 1970s, chefs from around the world (and the need to offer familiar ingredients and dishes to expats from as far afield as Beijing and Berlin) have seasoned a once-bland dining scene.

Today, despite its small size, comparative isolation, and British colonial trappings, Grand Cayman offers a smorgasbord of gastronomic goodies. With more than 100 eateries, something should suit and sate every palate and pocketbook (especially once you factor in fast-food franchises sweeping the islandscape like tumbleweed and stalls dispensing local specialties).

The term *melting pot* describes both the majority of menus and the multicultural population. It's not uncommon to find "American" dishes at an otherwise Caribbean restaurant, Indian fare at an Italian eatery (and vice versa). The sheer range of dining options from Middle Eastern to Mexican reflects the island's cosmopolitan, discriminating clientele. Imported ingredients reflect the United Nations, with chefs sourcing salmon from Norway, foie gras from Périgord, and lamb from New Zealand. Wine lists can be equally global in scope (often receiving awards from such oeno-bibles as *Wine Spectator*). Don't be surprised to find both Czech and Chilean staffers at a remote East End restaurant.

As one restaurateur quipped, "Cayman is the ultimate culture-shock absorber."

WHERE TO EAT

Grand Cayman dining is casual (even shorts are okay, at least for lunch, but *not* beachwear and tank tops). More upscale restaurants usually require slacks for dinner. Mosquitoes can be pesky when you dine outdoors, especially at sunset, so plan ahead or ask for repellent. Winter can be chilly enough to warrant a light sweater. You should make reservations at all but the most casual places, particularly during the high season.

CLOSE UP

Eat Like a Local

Caymanian cuisine evolved from whatever could be coaxed from the sea and eked out from the poor, porous soil. Farmers cultivated carb-rich crops that could remain fresh without refrigeration and furnish energy for the heavy labor typical of the islanders' hardscrabble existence. Hence pumpkins, coconuts, plantains, breadfruit, sweet potatoes, yams, and other "provisions" (root vegetables) became staple ingredients. Turtle (now farm-raised), the traditional specialty, can be served in soup or stew and as a steak. Conch, the meat of a large pink mollusk, is prepared in stews, chowders, and fritters and panfried (cracked). Fish—including snapper, tuna, wahoo, grouper, and marlin—is served baked, broiled, steamed, or "Cayman-style" (as an *escovitch* with peppers, onions, and tomatoes).

"Rundown" is another classic:

Fish (marinated with fresh lime juice, scallions, and fiery Scotch bonnet peppers) is steamed in coconut milk with breadfruit, pumpkin dumplings, and/ or cassava. Fish tea boils and bubbles similar ingredients for hours—even days—until it thickens into gravy. The traditional dessert, heavy cake, earned its name because excluding scarce flour and eggs made it incredibly dense: Coconut, sugar, spices, and butter are boiled, mixed with seasonal binders (cassava, yam, pumpkin), and baked.

Jamaican influence is seen in oxtail, goat stew, jerk chicken and pork, salt cod, and ackee (a red tree fruit resembling scrambled eggs in flavor and texture when cooked), and manish water (a lusty goat-head stew with garlic, thyme, scallion, green banana [i.e., plaintain], yam, potato, and other tubers).

Since nearly everything must be imported, prices average about 25% higher than those in a major U.S. city. Many restaurants add a 10%–15% service charge to the bill; be sure to check before leaving a tip (waiters usually receive only a small portion of any included gratuities, so leave something extra at your discretion for good service). Alcohol can send your meal tab skyrocketing. Buy liquor dutyfree, either at the airport before your flight to the Cayman Islands or in one of the duty-free liquor stores that can be found in almost every strip mall on Grand Cayman, and enjoy a cocktail or nightcap from the comfort of your room or balcony. Cayman customs limits you to two bottles per person. Lunch often offers the same or similar dishes at a

BEST BETS

Fodor's Choice ★
Agua, Blue by Eric Ripert,
Grand Old House, Luca, Michael's Genuine, Mizu, Ortanique, Ragazzi

BEST VIEWS
Cracked Conch, Grand Old
House, Luca, Morgan's Har-
bour, Osetra Bay, Over the
Edge, Reef Grill at Royal
Palms

BEST FOR ROMANCE
Beach House, Blue by Eric
Ripert, Grand Old House, Mizu,

Reef Grill at Royal Palms

BEST FOR FAMILIES
Al La Kebab, Chicken!
Chicken!, Cimboco, Eats Café

BEST FOR LOCAL CUISINE
Chicken! Chicken!, Cimboco,
Over the Edge, Vivine's
Kitchen

MOST POPULAR
Agua, Al La Kebab, Eats Café,
Guy Harvey's Island Grill, Mor-
gan's Harbour, Ragazzi, The
Waterfront, Yoshi Sushi

considerable discount. Finally, when you are figuring your dining budget, remember that the Cayman dollar is worth 25% more than the U.S. dollar, and virtually all menus are priced in Cayman dollars.

WHAT IT COSTS IN U.S. DOLLARS			
$	$$	$$$	$$$$
Restaurants under $12	$12–$20	$21–$30	over $30

Restaurant prices are the average cost of a main course at dinner or, if dinner is not served, at lunch. Hotel prices are the lowest cost of a standard double room in high season.

GEORGE TOWN AND ENVIRONS

You'll find a fair number of restaurants in George Town, including such standbys as Guy Harvey's and Casanova, not to mention the splurge-worthy Grand Old House.

$$$$ ✕ **The Brasserie.** *Eclectic.* Actuaries, bankers, and CEOs frequent this contemporary throwback to a colonial country club for lunch and "attitude adjustment" happy hours for creative cocktails and complimentary canapés. Inviting fusion cuisine, emphasizing local ingredients whenever possible (the restaurant even has its own boat and garden), includes terrific bar tapas like chipotle-braised oxtail taco with pepper aioli and pickled vegetables, or melted Brie with

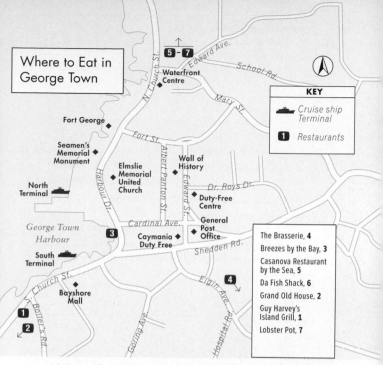

Where to Eat in George Town

KEY

Cruise ship Terminal

1 Restaurants

The Brasserie, **4**

Breezes by the Bay, **3**

Casanova Restaurant by the Sea, **5**

Da Fish Shack, **6**

Grand Old House, **2**

Guy Harvey's Island Grill, **1**

Lobster Pot, **7**

white truffle–and-mango marmalade. Several evenings, you can get a five- or eight-course market-driven "Random Acts of Cooking" blind tasting. Dishes deftly balance flavors and textures without sensory overload: this is serious food with a sense of playfulness. Save room for desserts, from an artisanal cheese plate to an ice-cream-and-sorbet tasting menu to elaborate architectural confections. Lunch is more reasonably priced but equally creative; the adjacent Market excels at takeout, and the wine list is well considered. $ *Average main: $34* ⊠ *171 Elgin Ave., Cricket Sq., George Town, Grand Cayman* ☎ *345/945–1815* ⊕ *www.brasseriecayman. com* ⚑ *Reservations essential* ⊙ *Closed weekends.*

$$ ✗ **Breezes by the Bay.** *Caribbean.* There isn't a bad seat in the house at this nonstop fiesta festooned with tiny paper lanterns, Christmas lights, ship murals, model boats, and Mardi Gras beads (you're "lei'd" upon entering). Wraparound balconies take in a dazzling panorama from South Sound to Seven Mile Beach. It's happy hour all day every day, especially during Countdown to Sunset. Signs promise "the good kind of hurricanes," referring to the 23-ounce signature "category 15" cocktails with fresh garnishes. Chunky, velvety conch chowder served in a bread bowl or

conch fritters are meals in themselves. Hefty sandwiches are slathered with jerk mayo or garlic aioli. Signature standouts include meltingly moist whole fish escovitch, popcorn shrimp, sliders, and any pie from the pizza station. ⑤ *Average main: $18* ⊠ *Harbor Dr., George Town, Grand Cayman* ☎ *345/943–8439* ⊕ *www.breezesbythebay.com* ⊘ *No dinner May–Sept.*

FREELOADING UP. Competition is fierce between Grand Cayman's many bars and restaurants. In addition to entertainment (from fish feeding to fire eating), even upscale joints host happy hours offering free hors d'oeuvres and/or drinks.

$$$$ ✕ **Casanova Restaurant by the Sea.** *Italian.* Owner Tony Crescente and younger brother–maitre d' Carlo offer a genuinely simpatico dining experience, practically exhorting you to *mangia*, and sending you off with a chorus of ciaos. The kitchen serves sterling Italian favorites like salmon marinated in citrus, olive oil, and basil; lemony veal piccata; gnocchetti in velvety four-cheese sauce with a blush of tomato; or seafood grill in parsley-garlic-lemon sauce. Enjoy grappa at the marble bar of Il Bacio lounge, which is lined with wooden wine racks (the impressive selection isn't overly Italian-centric). The patio juts over the harbor; the moonlight (abetted by a sound track of Bocelli to Bennett) would transform any amorous coward into a Casanova. ⑤ *Average main: $31* ⊠ *65 N. Church St., George Town, Grand Cayman* ☎ *345/949–7633* ⊕ *www.casanova. ky* ⌢ *Reservations essential.*

WORD OF MOUTH. "[Grand Cayman] is not a cheap place, but it is one of our favorite islands to eat on. When we were there, we grabbed a free *What's Hot* magazine. It tells you what's going on when you're on the island—and every once in awhile you might find a restaurant that has a deal. We absolutely love Casanova's. The Reef Grill also has a good menu and food.—Knowing.

$$ ✕ **Da Fish Shack.** *Seafood.* This classic clapboard seaside shanty couldn't be homier: constructed from an old fishing vessel, the structure is an authentic representation of original Caymanian architecture. The deck couldn't be better placed to savor the breezes and water views, and the chill Caribbean vibe makes it feel like you're dining at a friend's home. The owners source fresh local ingredients wherever possible and developed relationships with Caymanian fishermen, who often cruise up to the dock with their catch. Savor jerk fish tacos, salt-fish fritters, coconut shrimp with pineapple tomato salsa, and golden crunchy breadfruit fries. A wide array of non-seafood dishes are offered, from chicken schnitzel to a rib eye with sauce chasseur. The place hops on "Sundown Saturdays" with a CI$20 waterfront barbecue. Free Wi-Fi and occasional DJs are bonuses. ⑤ *Average main: $16* ⊠ *127 N. Church St., George Town, Grand Cayman* ☎ *345/947–8126* ⊕ *www. dafishshack.com.*

★ **Fodor'sChoice** ✕ **Grand Old House.** *European.* Built in 1908 **$$$$** as the Petra Plantation House and transformed into the island's first upscale establishment decades ago, this grande dame is that rare restaurant that evokes bygone grandeur sans pretension. The interior rooms, awash in crystal, recall its plantation-house origins. Outside, hundreds of sparkling lights adorn the gazebos to compete with the starry sky. Live nightly music and rumors of a charming blond ghost trailing white chiffon complete the picture: this is a place to propose. You'll find expertly executed classics such as panfried foie gras with ice wine raspberry compote, broiled lobster tail with smoked bell-pepper butter, or filet mignon with green peppercorn sauce. The subtle yet complex flavor interactions, stellar service, and encyclopedic if stratospherically priced wine list ensure legendary landmark status. Nightly happy hours with discounted tapas are a sensational bargain. ⑤ *Average main: $56* ⊠ *648 S. Church St., George Town, Grand Cayman* ☎ *345/949–9333* ⊕ *www. grandoldhouse.com* ⌂ *Reservations essential* ⊘ *Closed Sept. Closed Sun. in low season. No lunch weekends.*

$$$$ ✕ **Guy Harvey's Island Grill.** *Seafood.* At this stylish, sporty, upstairs bistro you half expect to find Hemingway regaling fellow barflies in the clubby interior with mahogany furnishings, ship's lanterns, porthole windows, fishing rods, and Harvey's action-packed marine art. The cool blues echo the sea and sky on display from the balcony. Seafood is carefully chosen to exclude overexploited and threatened species. Seasonally changing dishes are peppered with Caribbean influences but pureed through the French chef's formal training. Hence, silken lobster bisque is served with puff pastry, scallops Rockefeller with spinach and béarnaise sauce, and the signature crab cakes with roasted-red-pepper aioli. You can select your fish baked, pan-sautéed, or grilled with any of eight sauces. Carnivores needn't despair, with rack of lamb Provençale in balsamic glaze or an intensely flavored filet mignon Roquefort (frites optional). Many specialties are cheaper at lunch. Nightly specials for CI$9.99 and the four-course CI$30 dinner reel

CLOSE UP

Farm Fresh

A joint initiative of the Cayman Islands Agricultural Society, the Ministry of Agriculture, the Department of Agriculture, and local vendors-purveyors, the **Market at the Grounds** is a jambalaya of sights, sounds, and smells held every Saturday from 7 AM at the Stacy Watler Agricultural Pavilion in Lower Valley (East End). Local growers, fishers, home gardeners and chefs (dispensing scrumptious, cheap cuisine), and artisans display their wares in a tranquil green setting. To preserve Caymanian flavor, everything must be 100% locally grown. Participating craftspeople and artists, from couturiers to musicians, must use local designs and materials whenever possible. The market fosters a renewed spirit of community, providing literal feedback into the production process, while the interaction with visitors promotes understanding of island culture.

in savvy locals. ⑤ *Average main: $40* ⊠ *Aquaworld Duty-Free Mall, 55 S. Church St., George Town, Grand Cayman* ☎ *345/946–9000* ⊕ *www.guyharveysgrill.com.*

$$$$ ✕ **Lobster Pot.** *Seafood.* The nondescript building belies the lovely marine-motif decor and luscious seafood at the intimate, second-story restaurant overlooking the harbor. Enjoy lobster prepared several ways along with reasonably priced wine, which you can sample by the glass in the cozy bar. The two musts are the Cayman Trio (lobster tail, grilled mahimahi, and garlic shrimp), and the Pot (lobster, giant prawns, and crab). The kitchen happily provides reduced-oil and -fat alternatives to most dishes; vegetarians love such flavorful selections as chili-lime polenta with grilled artichoke in mango cream and roasted pumpkin, garlic, and thyme risotto. The recently enlarged balcony offers a breathtaking view of the sunset tarpon feeding. Lobster is market price and can be as much as $60; other entrées are less expensive. ⑤ *Average main: $45* ⊠ *245 N. Church St., George Town, Grand Cayman* ☎ *345/949–2736* ⊕ *www. lobsterpot.ky* ⊗ *No lunch Sat.*

SEVEN MILE BEACH

The lion's share of Grand Cayman restaurants is to be found along Seven Mile Beach, where most of the island's resorts are also located. Some are in the strip malls on the east side of West Bay Road, but many are in the resorts themselves.

★ Fodor's Choice ✕ **Agua.** *Italian.* This quietly hip spot plays up
$$$$ an aquatic theme with indigo glass fixtures, black-and-
white nautical photos, and cobalt-and-white walls subtly
recalling foamy waves. The team of young, international
chefs emphasize seafood, preparing regional dishes from
around the globe with a Caymanian slant. Thai ceviche
with Kaffir lime and coconut milk and tuna tiradito (similar to carpaccio) with avocado tamarind sauce burst with
flavor. Superlative pastas include buffalo mozzarella tor-
telli in basil butter and lobster-shiitake ravioli with potato
mascarpone sauce. Don't miss the authentic gelatos to cap
your meal. Wine selections from lesser-known regions often
represent good value, with 20 offered by the glass; the bartenders also creatively pair cocktails and food. Happy-hour
free tapas and the CI$19.95 three-course lunch menu are
steals. ⑤ *Average main: $36* ✉ *Galleria Plaza, Seven Mile
Beach, Grand Cayman* ☎ *345/949–2482* ⊕ *www.agua.ky*
⚑ *Reservations essential.*

$ ✕ **Al La Kebab.** *Middle Eastern.* The Silvermans started by
serving late-night kebabs and gyros, and now their eatery
works miracles out of two makeshift lean-tos splashed in
vibrant colors. They remain open until 4 am weeknights
and 2 am weekends. Alan calls it a building-block menu,
where you can modify the bread and sauce—a dozen vari-
eties, including several curries, peanut satay, mango *raita*
(yogurt, tomatoes, chutney), tahini, teriyaki, garlic cream,
even gravy like Mom used to make. The menu romps
from Malaysia through the Mediterranean to Mexico:
spicy chicken tikka, Thai chicken-lemongrass soup, and
tzatziki share the stage with unusual salads (try the fabulous Lebanese *fattoush*—toasted bread, mint, and parsley)
and creative sides (addictive jalapeño-cheddar salsa for
fries). ⑤ *Average main: $9* ✉ *Marquee Plaza, West Bay
Rd., Seven Mile Beach, Grand Cayman* ☎ *345/943–4343*
⊕ *www.kebab.ky* ⚑ *Reservations not accepted.*

$$$$ ✕ **The Beach House.** *Seafood.* This refined eatery (aka Casa
Havana) glamorously channels South Beach and Santa
Monica, with a sexy black bar dispensing luscious libations,
an earthy color scheme, and sparkly ecru curtains dividing
dining spaces. Executive Chef Michaell Farrell hails from
the Big Easy, and his food, which he dubs "coastal cuisine,"
travels from Nantucket to New Orleans with aplomb. The
menu offers mostly small plates, ideal for grazing, and
large plates to be shared family-style. Seafood is the star,
unsurprisingly. Witness the sea bass with lump crab and
apple-smoked bacon; seared scallop with fennel risotto and

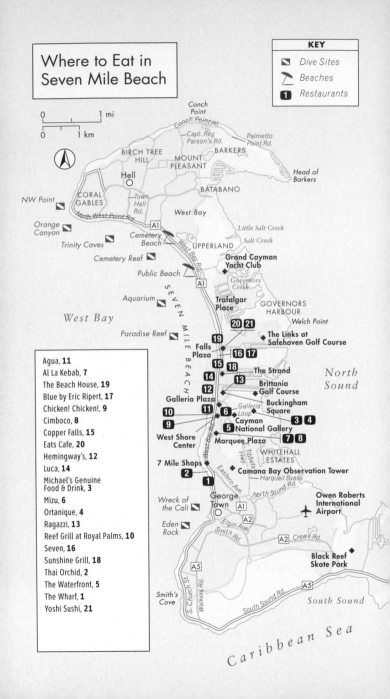

Where to Eat in Seven Mile Beach

KEY

◣ Dive Sites
↗ Beaches
1 Restaurants

Agua, **11**
Al La Kebab, **7**
The Beach House, **19**
Blue by Eric Ripert, **17**
Chicken! Chicken!, **9**
Cimboco, **8**
Copper Falls, **15**
Eats Cafe, **20**
Hemingway's, **12**
Luca, **14**
Michael's Genuine
Food & Drink, **3**
Mizu, **6**
Ortanique, **4**
Ragazzi, **13**
Reef Grill at Royal Palms, **10**
Seven, **16**
Sunshine Grill, **18**
Thai Orchid, **2**
The Waterfront, **5**
The Wharf, **1**
Yoshi Sushi, **21**

cassis demi-glace; or a lightly poached "butter" lobster with grapefruit-pepper emulsion. But carnivores needn't despair: The sous vide beef tenderloin practically dissolves in your mouth. Pairings are suggested for each dish on the menu; the wine list features several fine buys at $35, with some surprising high-end bargains. Wine Master dinners pair several courses with wines (Marchese di Barolo to Gosset champagne), often introduced by the guest winemakers or owners from as far afield as Tuscany, Australia, Napa, and Chile. ⑤ *Average main: $38* ⌧ *The Westin Grand Cayman Seven Mile Beach Resort & Spa, West Bay Rd., Seven Mile Beach, Grand Cayman* ☎ *345/945–3800* ⊕ *www.westin-grandcayman.com.*

★ **Fodor'sChoice** ✕ **Blue by Eric Ripert.** *Seafood. Top Chef* judge
$$$$ Eric Ripert's trademark ethereal seafood (executed by his handpicked brigade), flawless but not fawning service, swish setting, and soothing sophistication sans pretension make Blue one of the Caribbean's finest restaurants. Choose from a regular four-course or the chef's hedonistic six- and seven- course tasting menus (with or without wine pairing); there are also trendy "almost raw" and "barely touched" options. Many dishes are clever riffs on the mother restaurant (New York's celebrated Le Bernardin), using the island's natural bounty (the tribute to the great Bernardin tuna foie gras adds Cayman sea salt). Sensuous options include sautéed kingklip with avocado-coconut cream, sunflower sprouts, and lime sauce *vierge,* melt-in-your-mouth chocolate mousse with caramelized banana, mango-saffron sauce, and cocoa sorbet. The vast wine list offers quality and comparative value. ⑤ *Average main: $119* ⌧ *Ritz-Carlton Grand Cayman, West Bay Rd., Seven Mile Beach, Grand Cayman* ☎ *345/943–9000* ⚐ *Reservations essential* ⊘ *Closed Sun. and Mon. No lunch.*

$$ ✕ **Chicken! Chicken!.** *Caribbean.* Chicken! Chicken! Devo-
FAMILY tees would probably award four exclamation points to the marvelously moist chicken, slow-roasted on a hardwood open-hearth rotisserie. Most customers grab takeout, but the decor is appealing for a fast-food joint; the clever interior replicates an old-time Cayman cottage. Bright smiles and home cooking completely from scratch enhance the authentic vibe. Hearty but (mostly) healthful heaping helpings of sides include scrumptious Cayman-style corn bread, honey-rum beans, jicama coleslaw, and spinach-pesto pasta. Prices are even cheaper at lunch. ⑤ *Average main: $12* ⌧ *West Shore Centre, West Bay Rd., Seven Mile Beach, Grand Cayman* ☎ *345/945–2290* ⊕ *www.chicken2.com.*

$$ ✕ **Cimboco.** *Eclectic.* This animated space celebrates all things fun and Caribbean with walls saturated in orange, lemon, and lavender; cobalt glass fixtures; and flames dancing up the exhibition kitchen's huge wood-burning oven. The *Cimboco* was the first motorized sailing ship built in Cayman (in 1927) and for 20 years the lifeline to the outside world; National Archive photographs and old newspapers invest the space with still more character. Everything from breads (superlative bruschetta and jalapeño corn bread) to ice creams is made from scratch. Artisanal pizzas come with toppings such as balsamic-roasted eggplant, pesto, and feta; or curried chicken with pineapple and spinach. Signature items include banana-leaf-roasted snapper and fire-roasted bacon-wrapped shrimp. Amazingly good desserts include a sinfully rich brownie. The popular breakfast and brunch are equally creative. $ *Average main: $19* ✉ *The Marquee, West Bay Rd. at Harquail Bypass, Seven Mile Beach, Grand Cayman* ☎ *345/947–2782* ⊕ *www.cimboco.com.*

$$$$ ✕ **Copper Falls.** *Steakhouse.* The restaurant's tagline, "A Rare Steakhouse, Very Well Done," is only a touch hyperbolic. The brashly contemporary look (copper-clad waterfalls and hand-painted metal bas relief contrasting with century-old Douglas fir wainscoting and high-back suede booths) screams corporate takeover in progress. Hand-cut 28-day aged Angus cuts, from 8-ounce filet mignon to 28-ounce porterhouse, certify its Grade A status, attracting a demanding business clientele. Lighter options run from red snapper topped with lobster and mushrooms in sun-dried tomato sauce to Parmesan-Dijon mustard-crusted chicken with garlic demi-glace. There's a choice of five starches (including scrumptious garlic mashed potatoes), three vegetables, and six sauces. Best of all, every entrée includes a complimentary beer or cocktail (the martinis would stir 007), helping make Copper Falls pure gold for steak-house purists. $ *Average main: $52* ✉ *43 Canal Point Rd., The Strand, Seven Mile Beach, Grand Cayman* ☎ *345/945–4755* ⊕ *www.copperfallssteakhouse.com* ⌕ *Reservations essential* ⊘ *Closed Mon. Sept. and Oct. No lunch.*

$$ ✕ **Eats Cafe.** *Eclectic.* This happy, hopping hangout is more
FAMILY eclectic and stylish than any diner, with dramatic decor (crimson booths and walls, flat-screen TVs lining the counter, pendant steel lamps, an exhibition kitchen, gigantic flower paintings, and Andy Warhol reproductions) and vast menu (Cajun to Chinese), including smashing breakfasts. The 10-plus burgers alone (Rasta Mon Jerkya to Smokey Mountain BBQ, as well as fish and veggie versions) could

satisfy almost any craving, but you could also get a Caesar salad or sushi, Philly cheese steak or chicken chimichangas or curries. It's noisy, busy, buzzing, and hip—but not aggressively so. ⑤ *Average main: $16* ✉ *Falls Plaza, West Bay Rd., Seven Mile Beach, Grand Cayman* ☎ *345/943–3287* ⊕ *www.eats.ky.*

$$$$ ✕ **Hemingway's.** *Eclectic.* Willowy palms, hardwood furnishings, a churchlike profusion of candles and torches, whirring paddle fans, wicker, lacquered bamboo, and picture windows opening onto Seven Mile Beach pay tribute to Hemingway's tropical travels. The new menus add an intriguing Asian gloss to the preparations, though seafood is the standby from cioppino to the oyster trilogy to an aquatic tapas sampler. Fish can be prepared to your preference, with a choice of sauces (citrus salsa, tamarind chutney, spicy creole, pico de gallo, jerk tropical salsa, ginger soy reduction, and passion-fruit beurre blanc). The key lime pie does justice to the restaurant's namesake. Saturday night live jazz is extremely popular. ⑤ *Average main: $34* ✉ *Grand Cayman Beach Suites, West Bay Rd., Seven Mile Beach, Grand Cayman* ☎ *345/945–5700, 345/949–1234* ⊕ *www. grand-cayman-beach-suites.com* ⌂ *Reservations essential.*

★ **Fodor'sChoice** ✕ **Luca.** *Italian.* Owners Paolo Polloni and Andi
$$$$ Marcher spared no expense in realizing their vision of a smart beachfront trattoria that wouldn't be out of place in L.A. Everything was painstakingly handpicked, from the wine "wall" of more than 3,000 bottles from around the globe to the Murano glass fixtures, leather banquettes, and a curving onyx-top bar. Chef Frederico Destro delights in unorthodox pairings, all gorgeously presented. Tuna is served with pea pesto, wild rice, and Scotch bonnet aioli. Hudson Valley foie gras knits poached apple with sherry reduction and onion fondue, but the standout entrée is a delicious whole Mediterranean striped bass baked in salt crust. ⑤ *Average main: $46* ✉ *Caribbean Club, 871 West Bay Rd., Seven Mile Beach, Grand Cayman* ☎ *345/623–4550* ⌂ *Reservations essential* ⊘ *Closed Mon. Sept. and Oct. No lunch Sat.*

★ **Fodor'sChoice** ✕ **Michael's Genuine Food & Drink.** *Eclectic.* James
$$$$ Beard Award–winning chef Michael Schwartz and handpicked original executive chef Thomas Tennant successfully imported the slow-food philosophy of the groundbreaking Michael's Genuine in Miami. Seasonal menu items come from the on-site garden, and from carefully chosen Cayman farmers, fishermen, and ranchers. The results live up to the Schwartz mantra of "fresh, simple, pure": honest, unclut-

tered food. Lunch offers a more traditional but lengthy selection, whereas dinner dishes come in small, medium, and large portions: perfect for family sharing. The ever-changing menu includes burrata and crispy sweet-and-sour pork belly, and wood-oven-roasted dishes like pizza, snapper, or *poulet rouge* chicken. The well-considered wine list offers occasional bargains. Tennant had also devised an inspired solution to the invasive lionfish population: look for it as a menu special, and if you dive, ask about the Lionfish Safari. Ⓢ *Average main: $39* ✉ *47 Forum La., Canella Court, Camana Bay, Grand Cayman* ☎ *345/640–6433* ⊕ *www.michaelsgenuine.com.*

★ **Fodor's**Choice ✕ **Mizu.** *Asian.* It's a toss-up as to which is sexier
$$$ at this pan-Pacific bistro: the sleek decor, the model-worthy waitstaff, or the glistening, artfully presented food. The former, courtesy of Hong Kong designer Kitty Chan, is as sensuous as a 21st-century opium den with a back-lighted dragon, contemporary Buddhas, glowing granite bar, and enormous mirrors. The bartenders have developed a loyal local following for their flair in more ways than one. The latter trots effortlessly all over Asia for culinary inspiration: terrific tuna tartare, decadent duck gyoza, killer kung pao chicken, smashing Singapore fried noodles, heavenly honey-glazed ribs, beautifully crispy Okinawan-style pork belly, and two dozen ultra-fresh maki (try the signature roll). An extensive tea selection and a sake and wine list are also offered. Ⓢ *Average main: $24* ✉ *Camana Bay, Grand Cayman* ☎ *345/640–0001* ⊕ *www.mizucayman.com.*

★ **Fodor's**Choice ✕ **Ortanique.** *Eclectic.* The vibrant food at Orta-
$$$$ nique lives up to its nickname, "Cuisine of the Sun." It's an outpost of chef Cindy Hutson and Delius Shirley's Miami Ortanique, which helped revolutionize Floribbean fusion fare. The interior gleams in rich yellows and oranges that subtly recall plantation living, though prize seating is on the patio, shaded by sea grape trees overlooking a small islet. There is an emphasis on Caribbean and South American cuisine infused with Asian inspirations. Executive Chef Sara Mair, a semifinalist on *Top Chef*, reinvents classics with an island twist: jerk-rubbed foie gras with burnt-orange marmalade, or the signature jerked double pork chop, fire-tamed by guava-spiced rum glaze. Save room for such decadent desserts as a deceptively airy Cloud of Coconut Joy or rum-soaked banana fritters. Best of all are almost nightly specials from Mojito Madness Mondays to Tapas Thursdays. Ⓢ *Average main: $42* ✉ *47 Forum La., The*

Crescent, Camana Bay, Grand Cayman ☎ *345/640–7710* ⊕ *www.ortaniquerestaurants.com.*

★ **Fodor's**Choice ✕ **Ragazzi.** *Italian.* The name means "good bud-
$$$ dies," and this strip-mall jewel is always percolating with
conversation and good strong espresso. The airy space is
convivial: blond woods, periwinkle walls and columns, and
handsome artworks of beach scenes, sailboats, and palm
trees. Chef Adriano Usini turns out meticulously prepared
standards. The antipasto alone is worth a visit, as are the
homemade bread sticks and focaccia, and definitive carpac-
cio and insalata Caprese. The shellfish linguine in a light,
silken tomato sauce, with cherry-tomato skins pulled back
and crisped, and gnocchi in four-cheese sauce with brandy
and pistachios will please any pasta perfectionist. Two
dozen first-rate pizzas emerge from the wood-burning oven,
and meat and seafood mains are beautifully done, never
overcooked. The wine list is notable (400-odd choices) for
a casual eatery, showcasing great range and affordability
even on high-ticket, hard-to-find heavy hitters such as
Biondi Santi Brunello, Jermann Pinot Grigio, and Giacosa
Barbaresco; the knowledgeable staff will gladly suggest
pairings. ⑤ *Average main: $29* ⊠ *Buckingham Sq., West Bay
Rd., Seven Mile Beach, Grand Cayman* ☎ *345/945–3484*
⊕ *www.ragazzi.ky.*

$$$$ ✕ **Reef Grill at Royal Palms.** *Eclectic.* This class act appeals
to a casual, suave crowd, many of them regulars, who
appreciate its consistent quality, efficient service, soothing
seaside setting, top-notch entertainment, and surprisingly
reasonable prices. The space is cannily divided into four
areas, each with its own look and feel, including private
beach cabanas (no extra charge). Co-owner–chef George
Dahlstrom gives his perfectly prepared, familiar items just
enough twist to satisfy jaded palates: calamari is fried in
arborio rice batter with jalapeño aioli while sea scallops
are pan-seared with a creamy roasted corn–smoked bacon
mash. The Royal Palms menu offers more casual, inexpen-
sive fare. Dance the calories off to the estimable reggae,
calypso, and soca sounds of Coco Red or really sweat it
out during Chill Wednesdays, and then adjourn to the cozy
lounge for an aged rum or single malt. It's equally entic-
ing at lunch, when it exudes a soigné beach bar ambience.
⑤ *Average main: $33* ⊠ *537 West Bay Rd., Seven Mile
Beach, Grand Cayman* ☎ *345/945–6358* ⊕ *www.reefgrill.
com* ⊘ *No dinner Sun. May–Nov.*

$$$$ ✕ **Seven.** *Steakhouse.* The Ritz-Carlton's all-purpose dining
room transforms from a bustling breakfast buffet into an

elegant eatery come evening. Tall potted palms, soaring ceilings, black and beige color scheme, twin wine walls bracketing a trendy family-style table, and the tiered pool just outside are lighted to strategically stylish effect. Sinatra and Ella keep the sultry beat while the kitchen jazzes standard meat-and-potatoes dishes with inventive seasonings and eye-catching presentations. Splendid aged Niman Ranch steaks come with five sauces and rubs, from five-peppercorn to béarnaise. Even such sides as truffled mac-and-cheese redefine divine decadence. The calorie- and cholesterol-conscious can savor melt-in-your-mouth ahi tuna poke or impeccably cooked Dover sole with hazelnut brown butter. Then just surrender to such confections as chocolate and sea salt caramel candy bar. ⑤ *Average main: $54* ⊠ *Ritz-Carlton Grand Cayman, West Bay Rd., Seven Mile Beach, Grand Cayman* ☎ *345/943–9000* ⊕ *www.ritzcarlton.com.*

$$ ✕ **Sunshine Grill.** *Caribbean.* This cheerful, cherished locals'
FAMILY secret serves haute comfort food at bargain-basement prices. Even the chattel-style poolside building, painted a delectable lemon with lime shutters, whets the appetite. Sunshine ranks high in the island's greatest burger debate, while the chicken egg rolls with mango chutney and jerk mayo and fabulous fish tacos elevate pub grub to an art form. Wash it down with one of the many signature libations, like the Painkiller. Take advantage of affordably priced nightly dinner specials such as red snapper amandine in lemon butter caper sauce, and Cuban roast chicken marinated with sour orange, garlic, lime, and olive oil. ⑤ *Average main: $18* ⊠ *Sunshine Suites, 1465 Esterley Tibbetts Hwy., Seven Mile Beach, Grand Cayman* ☎ *345/949–3000, 345/946–5848.*

$$$ ✕ **Thai Orchid.** *Thai.* East meets West at this elegant eatery, and the combination makes for a tasty meal. The look juxtaposes some Thai crafts and black-lacquer accents with track lighting, blue-pomegranate-and-mango sponge-painted walls, gilt-trim flower paintings, and bold artworks of semi-abstract beach scenes and decidedly Western cupids. The Thai chefs turn out splendid classics like *yum nuer* (sliced char-grilled strip loin tossed with green salad in lime dressing); the standout signature entrée is boneless duck sautéed with basil and bell peppers in chili sauce. Seafood lovers can opt for the fresh sushi, and plentiful vegetarian options include curries perfumed with lemongrass. Sunday's all-you-can-eat Thai–sushi buffet (just CI$19.95) is a bargain. Desserts return West, besting most Asian restaurants: dark-and-white-chocolate mousse cake with *crème anglaise*

CLOSE UP

Culinary Quality Control

In more than a decade at the helm of New York's Le Bernardin, sometime *Top Chef* panelist Eric Ripert has garnered every gastronomic accolade. Born in Antibes on the French Riviera, Ripert apprenticed at Parisian institution La Tour d'Argent and Joël Robuchon's Jamin, then worked stateside with Jean-Louis Palladin and David Bouley before Le Bernardin reeled him in. He opened his first "name" restaurant, Blue by Eric Ripert, at the Ritz-Carlton Grand Cayman in 2005. Others have since followed.

The Caribbean wasn't on Ripert's radar, as he has told us, but "the resort owner, Michael Ryan, was in New York for dinner at Le Bernardin. He wanted to discuss the Ritz and me opening its signature restaurant. When I came down, he picked me up, put me on a boat to swim at Stingray City, loaded me with champagne, then came straight here to discuss business.... I loved it, felt confident because of his commitment to quality and service."

The greatest challenge was "the quality of the seafood, which sounds illogical, but most fish here comes frozen from the United States. We visited fishermen, created a network, to get fresh catch regularly. It's the only item the hotel allows cash for, so [executive chef Frederic Morineau]

carries a big wad! We fought passionately for the quality of the seafood, since that's one of my trademarks. And with so few farmers and growers on island... produce was even more challenging, but we found squash, salad greens, herbs."

"Trying to use what's already here inspires me," says Morineau. "It's cooking in the landscape.... I can now get lemongrass, thyme, mint, basil, papaya, mango, callaloo, sweet potatoes, good stew tomatoes, Scotch bonnet, and other peppers. I'm a big advocate of the locally produced Cayman sea salt." He encourages local purveyors, but paramount was persuading management to commit the funds for specialty products worth the price. "We work with a couple of commercial fishing boats that bring huge wahoo, ocean yellowtail, deep-water snapper from as far afield as Mexico.... So fresh and so beautiful, a pleasure to work with."

Ripert draws parallels to his Mediterranean upbringing. "It's a different feel and look, of course, as are the cooking ingredients and preparations. But both cultures place great emphasis on food as a key part of their lives and borrow from many heritages. And both cultures know how to relax and enjoy themselves!"

and raspberry coulis is a standout. ⑤ *Average main: $28* ✉ *Queens Court, West Bay Rd., Seven Mile Beach, Grand Cayman* ☎ *345/949–7955* ⊕ *www.thaiorchid.ky.*

$$ ✕ **The Waterfront.** *Diner.* The ultra-contemporary design, FAMILY incorporating industrial elements (exposed piping, raw timber, modular shelves, slate floors, accents salvaged from a tugboat) effectively counterpoints the warm down-home fare at this bustling glorified diner with a difference. Comfort food aficionados can launch into the splendid chicken and waffles, meat loaf, and splendid classic poutine. But the kitchen is also adept at sexier dishes, such as polenta-portobello burger with goat cheese or lime-chili tiger shrimp over pasta with feta and arugula. Whatever you order, finish it off with the enormous cinnamon bun (though it might finish you off for the day). ⑤ *Average main: $16* ✉ *The Crescent, Camana Bay, Grand Cayman* ☎ *345/640–0002* ⊕ *www.waterfrontcayman.com.*

$$$$ ✕ **The Wharf.** *Seafood.* The popularity of this large restaurant often leads to impersonal service and mediocre food. But the location, a series of elevated decks and Victorian-style gazebos in blue and white hugging the sea, is enviable and helps to explain its enduring appeal (wedding parties have their own pavilion, but celebrations of all sorts can overrun the place, including Salsa Tuesdays with lessons). The Ports of Call bar is a splendid place for sunset fanciers, and tarpon feeding off the deck is a nightly (9 pm) spectacle. Stick to simpler fare (creole-style marinated conch fritters with homemade tartar sauce, lobster baked with truffled Parmesan in champagne) and avoid anything sounding too pretentious. Chef Christian Reiter is Austrian and patriotic, so save room for dessert: warm toffee banana pudding, apple strudel, or the house version of a napoleon don't disappoint. ⑤ *Average main: $42* ✉ *43 West Bay Rd., Seven Mile Beach, Grand Cayman* ☎ *345/949–2231, 345/814–0179* ⊕ *www. wharf.ky* ⚑ *Reservations essential* ⊘ *No lunch.*

$$$ ✕ **Yoshi Sushi.** *Japanese.* Superlative sushi is served at this modish, modern locals' lair. Scarlet cushions, cherry pendant blown-glass lamps, leather-and-bamboo accents, fresh orchids, and maroon walls help create a sensuous, even charged vibe in the main room. The backlighted bar sees its share of carefree customers trying to manipulate their chopsticks after a few kamikaze sake bomber missions (plunging hot cups of sake into frosty Kirin beer). Savvy diners literally leave themselves in Yoshi's hands (the rolls and nightly special sushi "pizzas" are particularly creative), and the raw-phobic can choose from fine cooked items,

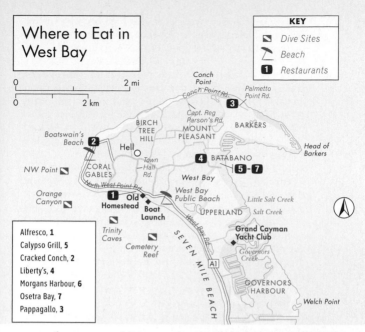

from tuna tataki to tempura to teriyaki. The congenial staff recommends intriguing sake and beer pairings, though the wine list and martini selection are also admirable for an Asian eatery. Ⓢ *Average main: $21* ✉ *Falls Plaza, West Bay Rd., Seven Mile Beach, Grand Cayman* ☎ *345/943–9674* ⊕ *www.eats.ky, www.legendz.ky* ✍ *Reservations essential.*

WEST BAY

There are fewer restaurant choices in West Bay, but there are some spots that are worth the trip. Be sure to have good driving directions when heading out into this area.

$$$ ✕ **Alfresco.** *Caribbean.* This ultrafriendly locals' insider spot, straddling the unofficial "border" between Seven Mile Beach and West Bay, resembles a little neighborhood diner transported to the ocean. Enjoy equally fresh sea breezes and food on the waterfront wood deck (built over a former parking lot) under one of the mismatched umbrellas. The co-owner is a longtime fisherman, and the fish-and-chips would make any Londoner proud. Other savvy seafood selections run from fiery Scotch bonnet shrimp to specials such as lobster ravioli in gossamer pumpkin-cream sauce.

Indeed, the menu is as much Capri as Cayman, with yummy pizzas and fried calamari served with both jerk mayo and marinara sauce. ⑤ *Average main: $21* ⊠ *53 Town Hall Rd., West Bay, Grand Cayman* ☎ *345/947–2525.*

$$$$ ✕**Calypso Grill.** *Eclectic.* Shack chic describes this inviting split-level space splashed in Dr. Seuss primary colors that contrast with brick walls, hardwood furnishings, terra-cotta floors, trompe l'oeil shutters, and (real) French doors opening onto sweeping North Sound views. If the interior is like stepping into a Caribbean painting, the outdoor deck serenely surveying frigate birds watchfully circling fishing boats is a Winslow Homer canvas brought to life. George Fowler's menu rightly emphasizes fish hauled in at the adjacent dock, so fresh (and never overcooked) that it almost literally jumps from the plate. You'll never go wrong with the unvarnished catch of the day grilled, blackened, or sautéed. Though this is seafood turf, landlubbers can savor escargot bourguignonne, beef carpaccio, or a proper rack of lamb. End with the sticky toffee pudding. ⑤ *Average main: $43* ⊠ *Morgan's Harbour, West Bay, Grand Cayman* ☎ *345/949–3948* ⊕ *www.calypsogrillcayman.com* ⚑ *Reservations essential* ⊘ *Closed Mon.*

WORD OF MOUTH. "We had dinner at Calypso Grill—my wife had the grilled tiger shrimp—a bit overpriced but good nonetheless. I had the blackened tuna and crab cakes as an appetizer. This was probably the best meal we had on the island . . . . Both my wife's shrimp and my blackened tuna came with the same (great) micro shoestring fries and grilled asparagus." —DKG50

$$$$ ✕**Cracked Conch.** *Eclectic.* This island institution effortlessly blends upscale and down-home. The interior gleams from the elaborate light-and-water sculpture at the gorgeous mosaic-and-mahogany entrance bar to the plush booths with subtly embedded lighting. Take in the remarkable water views through large shutters, but for maximum impact, dine on the multitiered patio. Executive chef Gilbert Cavallaro reinvents familiar dishes to create such delectables as honey-jerk-glazed tuna tartar with tomato sorbet and crispy calamari with cardamom-marinated carrots and chipotle sauce. Stellar signature items include the conch chowder or ceviche, silken short rib ravioli with truffles and Parmesan foam, and mahimahi poached *sous vide* over cannellini emulsion drizzled with truffle oil. Locals flock to Sunday brunch, or they just hang out at the dockside Macabuca tiki bar (fab sunsets, sunset-hued libations),

Food Fêtes

Gastronomy is big business on Grand Cayman, as upmarket eateries bank on the tourist dollar. Increasingly popular culinary events introduce visitors to local culture while beefing up biz, especially off-season. Celeb chef Eric Ripert debuted "Caribbean Rundown" weekend in 2007 at his Blue by Eric Ripert in the Ritz-Carlton, including cooking classes, fishing trips, and gala dinners, *Top Chef* competitor Dale Levitzki in tow.

It was such a success that *Food & Wine* co-sponsors the subsequent editions—now called Cayman Cookout—every January, with even more top toques stirring the broth: a recipe for success in this case. Both fests benefit local charities. February's "A Taste of Cayman" has titillated taste buds for more than two decades, thanks to more than 30 participating restaurants, raffles, entertainment, and cook-offs.

which lives up to its mellow name, indigenous Taíno for "What does it matter?" ⑤ *Average main: $44* ✉ *Northwest Point Rd., West Bay, Grand Cayman* ☎ *345/945–5217* ⊕ *www.crackedconch.com.ky* ⊘ *Closed Sept.–mid-Oct. No lunch June–Nov.*

$$ ✕ **Liberty's.** *Caribbean.* Just follow the boisterous laughter and pulsating Caribbean tunes to this hard-to-find mint-green Caymanian cottage, where you feel like you've been invited to a family reunion. The Sunday Caribbean buffet attracts hordes of hungry churchgoers (call ahead to ensure they're open that week), but every day offers authentic turtle steak, oxtail, jerk, and delectable fried snapper with sassy salsas that liberate your taste buds from the humdrum. There's also a George Town outpost. ⑤ *Average main: $18* ✉ *140 Reverend Blackman Rd., West Bay, Grand Cayman* ☎ *345/949–3226.*

$$$$ ✕ **Morgans Harbour.** *Eclectic.* Energetic, effervescent Janie Schweiger patrols the front while husband Richard rules the kitchen at this simpatico seaside spot with smashing North Sound views. Locals and fishermen literally cruise into the adjacent dock for refueling of all sorts. You can sit in one of the cozy buildings decorated with Depression-era chandeliers and vivid aquatic artworks or admire the dexterous marine maneuverings from the interlocking decks. Richard's menu dances just as deftly from Asia to his Austrian home. Nimbly prepared nibbles include the wildly popular 10-ounce Brie-topped jerk burger and ceviche, but everything from chicken schnitzel to Thai seafood curry is

expertly cooked to order. Lunch offers several of the restaurant's greatest hits at even more palatable prices. Ⓢ *Average main: $32 ⊠ 4 Morgan's La., Morgan's Harbour, West Bay, Grand Cayman ☎ 345/946–7049 ⚑ Reservations essential.*

$$$$ ✕ Osetra Bay. *Eclectic.* Whether by day (when fishing boats as brightly colored as a child's finger painting trawl the tourmaline North Sound) or by night (when Cayman Kai's lights twinkle as the moon dapples the water with a thousand gold doubloons), the view alone guarantees a memorable meal. The design is almost as appetizing, from glowing columns strategically placed to flatter diners to the intimate, billowingly draped dining cabanas to the Starck-ish white-on-white ultralounges. Every element infuses the casual Caribbean underpinnings with a chic South Beach sensibility, literally bringing caviar to Cayman. The ever-changing, seasonal menu (sourced locally wherever possible) emphasizes seafood: blackened mahi with corn pancetta cream sauce and thyme fingerlings or tuna with fruit chutney, local string beans and beet puree—though vegetarians delight in the pastas, and carnivores can stake out dishes like the classic beef tartare or dry-aged rib eye. Ⓢ *Average main: $45 ⊠ Morgan's Harbour, West Bay, Grand Cayman ☎ 345/325–5000, 345/623–5100 ⊕ www.osetrabay.com ⚑ Reservations essential ⊘ No lunch Mon.–Sat. No dinner Sun.*

$$$$ ✕ Ristorante Pappagallo. *Italian.* Pappagallo, Italian for "parrot," hauntingly perches on the edge of a lagoon in a 14-acre bird sanctuary. Inside, riotously colored macaws, cockatoos, and parrots perch on swings behind plate glass, primping, preening, and practically commenting on the billing and cooing clientele. You feel like hacking through the luxuriant vegetation inside and out; the lost-in-the-jungle exoticism is enhanced by locally hewn stones, bamboo, homemade rope, and thatched palapas for outdoor seating. Yet the sleek deco-inspired black marble–and–polished brass accents bespeak the underlying seriousness. Italian-born Chef Marco Signori's food is definitely not for the birds, especially his sublime risotti and pastas and seafood such as mahimahi, the kick of its smoked chipotle emulsion balanced by the sweet and tart mango-papaya salsa. Be sure to thank Bogie, the African gray parrot, who really rules the roost. Ⓢ *Average main: $41 ⊠ Barkers, 444B Conch Point Rd., West Bay, Grand Cayman ☎ 345/949–1119 ⊕ www. pappagallo.ky ⚑ Reservations essential ⊘ No lunch.*

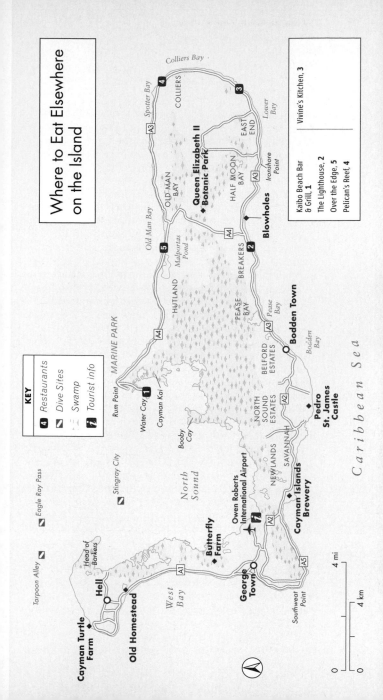

Where to Eat Elsewhere on the Island

KEY

- 🔳 **4** Restaurants
- 🔶 Dive Sites
- 🔳 Swamp
- 🔳 Tourist info

Kaibo Beach Bar & Grill, **1**
The Lighthouse, **2**
Over the Edge, **5**
Pelican's Reef, **4**

Vivine's Kitchen, **3**

Colliers Bay
Spotter Bay
4 COLLIERS
3
Lower Bay
EAST END
Queen Elizabeth II
◆ **Botanic Park**
HALF MOON BAY
Ironshore Point
OLD MAN BAY
Old Man Bay
◆ **Blowholes**
2
A3
A4
Malportas Pond
5
HUTLAND
BREAKERS
PEASE-BAY
Pease Bay
MARINE PARK
A4
A3
Rum Point
Water Cay
1
Cayman Kai
BELFORD ESTATES
Bodden Bay
Bodden Town ○
Booby Cay
NORTH SOUND ESTATES
◆ Pedro
St. James Castle
A2
North Sound
NEWLANDS
SAVANNAH
Stingray City
Owen Roberts International Airport
7
◆ **Butterfly Farm**
Cayman Islands Brewery ◆
A2
George Town ○
A1
A5
Southwest Point

Caribbean Sea

Eagle Ray Pass
Tarpoon Alley
Head of Barkers
Hell ○
◆ Old Homestead
Cayman Turtle Farm
West Bay

N

0
0   4 mi
     4 km

EAST END

While it can be at least a half-hour drive out here, some of the restaurants in East End are worth the trip from George Town.

$$$$ ✕ **The Lighthouse.** *Seafood.* This lighthouse surrounded by fluttering flags serves as a beacon for hungry East End explorers. The interior replicates a yacht: polished hardwood floors, ship's lanterns, mosaic hurricane lamps, steering wheels, portholes, and waiters in crew's garb with chevrons. Most tables afford sweeping sea vistas, but prize romantic seating is on the little deck. Starters include Miss Nell's red conch chowder or flash-fried calamari with sweet chili dip. Entrées include a platter of seafood floating on linguine alfredo and a mustard/herb-crusted rack of lamb with Marsala-mint sauce. Vegetarian options include curries, tofu stir-fries, and pastas. Save room for desserts, including the Illy espresso crème brûlée. The comprehensive wine list extends to a superb postprandial selection of liqueurs, aged rums, ports, and grappas. There are inexpensive prix fixe lunch and dinner specials CI$9.95 and CI $15, respectively). ⑤ *Average main: $35* ⊠ *Bodden Town Rd., Oceanside, Breakers, East End, Grand Cayman* ☎ *345/947–2047* ⊕ *www.lighthouse.ky.*

$$$$ ✕ **Pelican's Reef.** *Eclectic.* The Reef Resort's all-purpose dining room converts into a refined space come evening, its marine murals illuminated by candles, with clever partitioning by framed sails to enhance its intimacy. Most of the kitchen hails from the Caribbean, but even the buffets merrily marry culinary influences from India to Italy: they'll infuse hummus with saffron and spike spring rolls with wasabi. Everything uses the freshest produce. Occasional limbo contests and the iconic Barefoot Man's inimitable song stylings can alter the ambience from romantic to raucous. ⑤ *Average main: $39* ⊠ *Reef Resort, Colliers, East End, Grand Cayman* ☎ *345/947–3100* ⊕ *www.thereef.com* ⌂ *Reservations essential.*

$$ ✕ **Vivine's Kitchen.** *Caribbean.* Cars practically block the road at this unprepossessing hot spot for classic Caymanian food. You're literally eating in Vivine and Ray Watler's home; the prime seating is in the waterfront courtyard, where you will be serenaded by rustling sea grape leaves, crashing surf, and screeching gulls dive-bombing for their lunch. Daily changing menu items, all sourced locally to guarantee freshness, are scrawled on a blackboard: perhaps stewed turtle, curried goat, barbecued chicken, and snapper made to order, with cassava and sweet-potato cake sides. Burgers,

CLOSE UP

Eating at a Home Kitchen

Aspiring Anthony Bourdains on Grand Cayman should seek out roadside vans, huts, kiosks, and stalls dishing out unfamiliar grub that might unnerve wannabe *Survivor* contestants. These casual spots offer authentic fare at very fair prices, with main dishes and heaping helpings of sides costing under CI$10. If you thought Mickey D's special sauce or Coke was a secret formula, try prying prized recipes handed down for generations from these islanders.

Rankin's Jerk Centre. A faux cow and pig greet you at Rankin's Jerk Centre, where you can savor Miss Rankin's scrumptious turtle stew and jerk dishes in her alluring garden. ⊠ *3032 Shamrock Rd., Bodden Town, Grand Cayman* ☎ *345/947–3155.*

Chester's Fish Fry. Chester's Fish Fry has a devoted following for his jerk pork, fried fish, and downy fritters. ⊠ *563 Bodden Town Rd., Bodden Town, Grand Cayman* ☎ *345/939–3474.*

Two of these most casual eat-

eries on the island are George Town institutions.

Tony's Jerk Foods. Even politicos stand in line at Tony's Jerk Foods, which serves everything from cow foot to conch stew (you can't miss the exterior's beach mural). ⊠ *193 School Rd., George Town, Grand Cayman* ☎ *345/916–6860.*

Seymour's Jerk Centre. Seymour's Jerk Centre, in the parking lot of Roy's Boutique, is where island icon Seymour Silburn dishes out succulent slow-cooked smoky jerk (regulars have gotten their fix for more than two decades). ⊠ *Shedden Rd., George Town, Grand Cayman* ☎ *345/916–8531, 345/916–5418.*

Heritage Kitchen. West Bay's popular family-run Heritage Kitchen serves up legendary raconteur Tunny Powell's fish tea, barbecue ribs, and fish fry—with a generous portion of local lore. It's only open sporadically, so look for it when you're in the area. ⊠ *Just off Boggy Sand Rd., West Bay, Grand Cayman.*

3

dogs, and chicken-and-chips make a concession to more timid taste buds. Alcohol isn't served, but fresh tamarind, mango, and sorrel juices pack a flavorful punch. Vivine's generally closes early (and occasionally on Monday), but stays open if there's demand—and any food left. ⑤ *Average main: $17* ⊠ *Austin Dr., Gun Bay, East End, Grand Cayman* ☎ *345/947–7435* ▭ *No credit cards.*

NORTH SIDE

The North Side has a few good places to eat.

$$$ ✕ **Kaibo Beach Bar and Grill.** *Caribbean.* Spectacularly overlooking the North Sound, this quintessential beach hangout rocks days (fantastic lunches that cost half the price of dinner, festive atmosphere including impromptu volleyball tourneys, and free Wi-Fi), but serves murderous margaritas and mudslides well into the evening to a boisterous bevy of yachties, locals, sports buffs, and expats. Enjoy New England–style conch chowder with a hint of heat, smoked mahimahi pâté, hefty burgers, and wondrous wraps, either on the multitiered deck garlanded with ships' rope and Christmas lights or in hammocks and thatched cabanas amid the palms. The handsome, nautically themed Upstairs dining room swaddled in white muslin, open Thursday through Sunday nights (reservations essential), serves more creative fare at higher prices; specialties include baked grouper with Kaffir lime–leaf crust in lemongrass velouté. The ultimate in romance is the catered "Luna del Mar" evening hosted every Friday closest to the full moon. Tuesday beach barbecues are highly popular (including limbo dancing, live music, half-price drinks, and discounted water taxi service to the "mainland"). ⑤ *Average main: $30* ✉ *585 Water Cay Rd., Cayman Kai, North Side, Grand Cayman* ☎ *345/947–9975* ⊕ *www.kaibo.ky.*

$$$ ✕ **Over the Edge.** *Caribbean.* This fun, funky seaside spot brims with character and characters. (A soused regular might welcome you by reciting "the daily lunch special: chilled barley soup . That's beer.") The nutty nautical decor (brass ship's lanterns dangle from the ceiling, and steering wheels, lacquered turtle shells, and fishing photos adorn the walls) contrasts with cool mirrored ads for Gitanes and Mumm Cordon Rouge and the trendily semi-open kitchen with fresh fish prominently displayed. The jukebox jumps (country music rules the roost), and the tiki-lighted terrace offers stunning views and fresh breezes. Expertly prepared local fare (curried chicken to conch steak to Cayman rock lobster escovitch, served with rice and beans, plantains, and fried festival bread) is a bargain, especially at lunch, though the chef also surprises with such gussied-up fare as shrimp in Pernod sauce and turtle steak in port. ⑤ *Average main: $28* ✉ *Old Man Bay, North Side, Grand Cayman* ☎ *345/947–9568* ⊕ *www.over-theedge.com.*

WHERE TO STAY IN GRAND CAYMAN

By Jordan
Simon

Despite its small size, Grand Cayman offers a surprising range of accommodations: large luxury resorts, medium-size chain hotels, cozy condo enclaves, locally owned guesthouses—from boutique-y to budget, not to mention private villas.

The massive Ritz-Carlton resort on Seven Mile Beach was the first of several larger developments constructed under new laws allowing seven-story buildings. It was followed by the classy Caribbean Club Condominiums and the rebuilt upscale Beachcomber. Now high-rises sprout like fungi along Seven Mile Beach, each vowing and vying to be better—or at least grander—than the last.

Some of the acceptance of ever-grander development can be attributed to the lingering devastation of 2004's Hurricane Ivan, which totaled the island. The 230-room Hyatt Regency hotel, long the island standard-bearer, never recovered from the damage; Hyatt eventually withdrew from its last management responsibilities. For good or bad, Ivan provided many complexes with an excuse to renovate, even rebuild from the ground up and go ever higher. While the tacky, dilapidated condo enclaves were swept away, now practically every sizable lot of Seven Mile Beach is in various stages of development.

Brace yourself for resort prices—there are few accommodations in the lower-cost ranges in Grand Cayman. You'll also find no big all-inclusive resorts on Grand Cayman, and very few offer a meal plan of any kind. Happily, parking, at least, is always free at island hotels and resorts.

WHERE TO STAY

Seven Mile Beach is Boardwalk and Park Place for most vacationers. In a quirk of development, however, most of the hotels sit across the street from the beach (though they usually have beach clubs, bars, water-sports concessions, and other facilities directly on the sand). Most of Grand Cayman's condo resorts offer direct access to Grand Cayman's prime sandy real estate. Snorkelers should note that only the northern and southern ends of SMB feature spectacular reef development; the northern end is much quieter, so if you're looking for action, stay anywhere from the Westin Grand Cayman south, where all manner of restaurants and bars are walkable.

BEST BETS

Fodor's Choice ★
Caribbean Club, Cotton Tree, Lighthouse Point, Reef Resort, Ritz-Carlton Grand Cayman, Westin Grand Cayman

BEST BEACHFRONT
Coral Stone Club, Lacovia Condominiums, Reef Resort, Westin Grand Cayman

BEST FOR AN ECOFRIENDLY TRIP
Cobalt Coast, Compass Point, Lighthouse Point

BEST FOR FAMILIES
Ritz-Carlton Grand Cayman

BEST SERVICE
Reef Resort, Ritz-Carlton Grand Cayman

BEST FOR ROMANCE
Caribbean Club, Cotton Tree, Turtle Nest Inn

Tranquil **West Bay** retains the feel of an old-time fishing village; diving is magnificent in this area, but lodging options are limited, especially now that the long-promised Mandarin Oriental remains on indefinite hold.

Those who want to get away from it all should head to the bucolic **East End** and **North Side**, dotted with condo resorts and villas. The dive sites here are particularly pristine.

The **Cayman Kai/Rum Point**, starting at West Bay across the North Sound, offers the single largest concentration of villas and condo resorts, stressing barefoot elegance.

Hotel reviews have been shortened. For full information, visit Fodors.com.

WHAT IT COSTS IN U.S. DOLLARS				
	$	**$$**	**$$$**	**$$$$**
Hotels	under $275	$276–$375	$376–$475	over $475

Restaurant prices are the average cost of a main course at dinner or, if dinner is not served, at lunch. Hotel prices are the lowest cost of a standard double room in high season.

HOTELS AND RESORTS

Grand Cayman offers something for every traveler, with well-known chain properties in every price range and style. Accommodations run the gamut from outrageously deluxe to all-suites to glorified motor lodges. Add to that locally run hostelries that often offer better bang for the buck. Still, in a Caymanian quirk, condo resorts take up most of the prime beach real estate. And, with a couple of exceptions, hotels along Seven Mile Beach actually sit across the road from the beach.

B&BS, INNS, AND GUESTHOUSES

They may be some distance from the beach and short on style and facilities, or they may be surprisingly elegant, but all these lodgings offer a friendly atmosphere, equally friendly prices, and your best shot at getting to know the locals. Rooms are clean and simple at the very least, and most have private baths.

CONDOMINIUMS AND PRIVATE VILLAS

On Grand Cayman the number of available condos and villas greatly outnumbers hotel rooms. Most condos are very similar, with telephones, satellite TV, air-conditioning, living and dining areas, patios, and parking. Differences are the quality of in-condo amenities, facilities within their individual complexes (though pools, hot tubs, and barbecue grills are usually standard), proximity to town and the beach, and views. Some condos are privately owned and rented out directly by the owners; other complexes are made up solely of short-term rentals.

Grand Cayman's private villa rentals range from cozy one-bedroom bungalows to grand five-bedroom manses. Some stand completely independent; others may be located in a larger complex or enclave. While at first glance rental fees for villas may seem high, larger units can offer significant savings over hotels for families or couples traveling together. For example, if the cost of a three-bedroom villa is divided among three couples, the seemingly high nightly rental cost of $900 per night would only be $150 per person ($300 per couple); few hotels on Grand Cayman are so moderately priced. And, as in a condo, a full kitchen helps reduce the stratospheric price of dining out; a laundry room helps with cleanup, especially for families. Unless otherwise noted, all villas have landline phones, and local calls are usually free; phones are generally locked for international calls, though

Internet phone service could be included. Villa agents can usually help you rent a cell phone.

Rates are highest during the winter season from mid-December through mid-April. Most condo and villa rentals require a minimum stay, often five to seven nights in high season (during the Christmas holiday season the minimum will be at least one week and is sometimes two weeks, plus there are exorbitant fees). Off-season minimums are usually three to five nights.

Several of the condo- and villa-rental companies have websites where you can see pictures of the privately owned units and villas they represent; many properties are represented exclusively, others handled by several agents. In general, the farther north you go on Seven Mile Beach, the older and more affordable the property. Note also that many offices close on Sunday; if that's your date of arrival, they'll usually make arrangements for your arrival. There's often no maid service on Sunday either, as the island practically shuts down.

We no longer recommend individual private villas, especially since they frequently change agents. However, among the properties we've inspected worth looking for are Coral Reef, Venezia, Villa Habana, Great Escapes, Fishbones, and Pease Bay House.

VILLA AND CONDO RENTAL AGENTS

The **Cayman Islands Department of Tourism** (⊕ *www.caymanislands.ky*) provides a list of condominiums and small rental apartments. There are several condo and villa enclaves available on the beach, especially on the North Side near Cayman Kai, away from bustling Seven Mile Beach.

Quoted prices for villa and private condo rentals usually include government tax and often service fees (be sure to verify this). As a general rule of thumb, Seven Mile Beach properties receive daily maid service except on Sunday, but at villas and condos elsewhere on the island, extra services such as cleaning must be prearranged for an extra charge.

Cayman Island Vacations. Cayman Island Vacations was started by the affable couple Don and Linda Martin in 1989. Longtime Cayman homeowners, they represent more than 50 villas and condos (including their own). Extremely helpful with island suggestions, they can make arrangements for a rental car and extras. They arrange diving discounts, and Linda is one of Cayman's leading wedding coordinators. ☎*813/854–1201, 888/208–8935* ⊕*www.caymanvacation.com.*

Cayman Villas. Cayman Villas represents villas and condos on Grand Cayman and Little Cayman; from studios to six bedrooms with private pool. They'll gladly facilitate connections with potential staff from chefs to chauffeurs, recommend restaurants and tour operators, and even put you in touch with wedding coordinators. A great selling point: Every property has a manager, available 24/7 via cell phone, who lives on-site or nearby. They work with industry leader WIMCO. ☎*800/235–5888, 345/945–4144* ⊕*www.caymanvillas.com.*

Grand Cayman Villas. Grand Cayman Villas was started by Virginia resident Jim Leavitt, who carries listings for dozens of fine properties island-wide. He and his staff visit the island regularly to ensure quality and remain up-to-date with the latest development that might interest clients. ✉*Grand Cayman* ☎*866/358–8455* ⊕*www.grand-caymanvillas.net.*

Island Hideaways. Island Hideaways rents villas all over the Caribbean, including some in the Cayman Islands. ☎*800/832–2302* ⊕*www.islandhideaways.com.*

WIMCO. WIMCO, or the West Indies Management Company, is synonymous with quality throughout the world, especially the Caribbean. ☎*800/449–1553* ⊕*www.wimco.com.*

GEORGE TOWN AND ENVIRONS

If you are looking for a cheaper option and are willing to forego a beachfront location, there are a couple of guesthouses and simple hotels around George Town.

$ 🖵**Eldemire's Tropical Island Inn.** *B&B/Inn.* You're about 15 minutes from Seven Mile Beach at this guesthouse south of George Town, but less than 1 mile (1½ km) north of Smith Cove Beach. **Pros:** authentic Cayman hospitality and feel; inexpensive (with constant deals and discounts for paying cash); coin-operated laundry; free Wi-Fi. **Cons:** hard to find; slightly run-down; not on the beach. ⑤*Rooms from: $119* ✉*18 Pebbles Way, off S. Church St., Box 482, George Town, Grand Cayman* ☎*345/916–2022, 345/916–8369 Reservations, 704/468–2635 toll-free 9 am–9 pm from U.S.*

Market Watch

CLOSE UP

Most condo and villa rentals start on Saturday. Since all the island's major supermarkets (and most other stores) close on Sunday, condo and villa renters may want to stop off for essentials right after they pick up their rental car. There are several American-style supermarkets near the airport, along West Bay Road parallel to Seven Mile Beach, and elsewhere in the island; *for specific listings, see ⇨ Foodstuffs in Exploring Grand Cayman (with Shopping).* All stock fresh produce, poultry, and seafood; meats; baked goods; cold cuts and cheeses; hot and cold ready-made dishes at deli counters; and anything canned, frozen, and boxed. Just don't get sticker shock: Prices average 25%–30% more than at home. If you expect to arrive on a Sunday or holiday when the supermarkets are closed, ask the condo resort or rental agent to arrange a starter kit.

Cayman Vacation Shoppers. Cayman Vacation Shoppers is a godsend for advance provisioning; it's also the only outfit on the island permitted to deliver wine and spirits on Sunday. ☎ 345/916–2978 ⊕ www. caymanshoppers.com.

and Canada ⊕ www.eldemire.com ⟳ 4 rooms, 2 studios, 2 apartments ⫶⎸No meals.

$$ ⛨ **Sunset House.** *Hotel.* This amiable seaside dive-oriented resort is on the ironshore south of George Town, close enough for a short trip to stores and restaurants yet far enough to feel secluded. **Pros:** great shore diving and dive shop; lively bar scene; fun international clientele; great package rates. **Cons:** often indifferent service; somewhat run-down; no real swimming beach; spotty Wi-Fi signal. ⑤ *Rooms from: $290* ⊠ *390 S. Church St., George Town, Grand Cayman* ☎ *345/949–7111, 800/854–4767* ⊕ *www. sunsethouse.com* ⟳ *58 rooms, 2 suites* ⫶⎸*No meals.*

SEVEN MILE BEACH

Most travelers to Grand Cayman choose to stay on one of the resorts or condo complexes along beautiful Seven Mile Beach. While not all properties have a beachfront location, they are mostly in close proximity to the action and nearby restaurants, nightlife, and shops.

$$ ⛨ **The Anchorage.** *Rental.* Don't be deceived by the slightly dilapidated facade: this intimate resort's interiors were completely gutted and upgraded post-Ivan, and they're

DID YOU KNOW?

Seven Mile Beach is one of the Caribbean's most beautiful, and it's kept free from litter and pesky peddlers.

Caribbean Club

still a fine value. **Pros:** incredible vistas from George Town to West Bay from higher units; nice beach and snorkeling; Wi-Fi; great pool at the edge of the Caribbean. **Cons:** a bit isolated from action; boxy apartments. $ *Rooms from: $310* ✉ *1989 West Bay Rd., Box 30986, Seven Mile Beach, Grand Cayman* ☎ *345/945–4088* ⊕ *www.theanchoragecayman.com* ⮑ *15 2-bedroom condos* ⊙ *No meals.*

$$$ 🏨 **Aqua Bay Club.** *Rental.* One of the older condo complexes, ABC is scrupulously maintained, quiet, and affordable. **Pros:** great snorkeling very close to Cemetery Reef; friendly staff; free Wi-Fi and cell phone rental. **Cons:** beach can be rocky; no elevator in complex. $ *Rooms from: $430* ✉ *West Bay Rd., Seven Mile Beach, Grand Cayman* ☎ *345/945–4728, 800/825–8703* ⊕ *www.aquabayclub.com* ⮑ *21 1- and 2-bedroom units* ⊙ *No meals.*

★ Fodor'sChoice 🏨 **Caribbean Club.** *Rental.* This gleaming boutique facility includes a striking lobby filled with aquariums, a stunning infinity pool, and the contemporary trattoria, Luca. **Pros:** luxurious, high-tech facilities beyond the typical apartment complex; trendy Italian restaurant on-site; service on the beach. **Cons:** stratospheric prices; poor bedroom reading lights; though families are welcome, they may find it rather imposing; smaller balconies on top floor (albeit amazing views). $ *Rooms from: $1,256* ✉ *871 West Bay Rd., Seven Mile Beach, Grand Cayman* ☎ *345/623–4500, 800/941–1126* ⊕ *www.caribclub.com* ⮑ *37 3-bedroom condos* ⊙ *No meals.*

$$$$

$$ ⌕ **Christopher Columbus.** *Rental.* This enduring favorite on the
FAMILY peaceful northern end of Seven Mile Beach is a discovery
for families. **Pros:** excellent snorkeling; fine beach; great
value; free Wi-Fi. **Cons:** car really needed; often over-
run by families during holiday seasons and summer; top
floors feature splendid vistas but difficult access for physi-
cally challenged. ⓢ *Rooms from: $365* ✉ *2013 West Bay
Rd., Seven Mile Beach, Grand Cayman* ☎ *345/945–4354,
866/311–5231* ⊕ *www.christophercolumbuscondos.com*
⊸ *30 2- and 3-bedroom condos* ⊙ *No meals.*

$ ⌕ **Comfort Suites Grand Cayman.** *Hotel.* This no-frills, all-
suites hotel has an ideal location on West Bay Road, next
door to the Marriott and near numerous shops, restaurants,
and bars. **Pros:** affordable; nice complimentary extras like
buffet breakfast and Wi-Fi; fun young-ish crowd. **Cons:**
rooms nearly a block from the beach; new condominium
blocks sea views; no balconies; bar closes early. ⓢ *Rooms
from: $249* ✉ *West Bay Rd., George Town, Grand Cayman*
☎ *345/945–7300, 800/517–4000* ⊕ *www.caymancomfort.
com* ⊸ *108 suites* ⊙ *Breakfast.*

$$$$ ⌕ **Coral Stone Club.** *Rental.* This exclusive enclave shines in
the shadow of the Ritz-Carlton by offering understated
barefoot luxury, stellar service, and huge condos. **Pros:**
largest ratio of beach and pool space to guests; walking
distance to several restaurants and shops; free airport trans-
fers; excellent off-season deals. **Cons:** expensive in high
season; Ritz-Carlton guests sometimes wander over from
their packed section of sand trying to poach beach space.
ⓢ *Rooms from: $800* ✉ *West Bay Rd., Seven Mile Beach,
Grand Cayman* ☎ *345/945–5820, 888/927–2322* ⊕ *www.
coralstoneclub.com* ⊸ *30 3-bedroom condos* ⊙ *No meals.*

$ ⌕ **Discovery Point Club.** *Rental.* This older but upgraded
FAMILY complex of all oceanfront suites sits at the north end of
Seven Mile Beach, 6 mile (9½ km) from George Town,
with fabulous snorkeling in the protected waters of nearby
Cemetery Reef. **Pros:** sensational snorkeling; caring staff;
family-friendly; free Internet. **Cons:** car necessary to dine
out and explore; beach entry is rocky in spots; studios are
nothing but overpriced, glorified hotel rooms; no elevator.
ⓢ *Rooms from: $260* ✉ *West Bay Rd., Seven Mile Beach,
Grand Cayman* ☎ *345/945–4724, 866/384–9980* ⊕ *www.
discoverypointclub.com* ⊸ *37 1- and 2-bedroom condos*
⊙ *No meals.*

$$$$ ⌕ **Grand Cayman Beach Suites.** *Resort.* The former Hyatt all-
suites section, now locally run, offers a terrific beachfront
location and trendy eateries. **Pros:** fine beach; superior

4

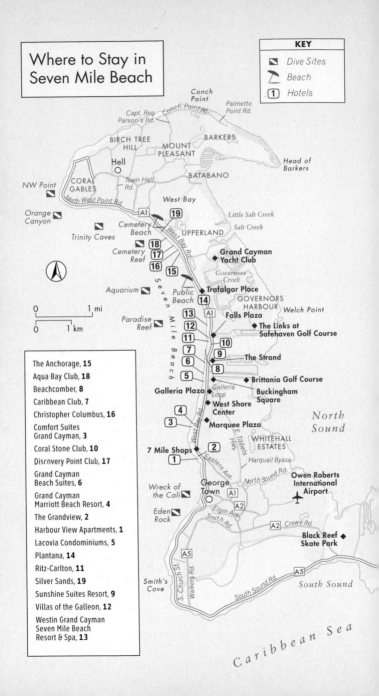

Where to Stay in Seven Mile Beach

KEY

- ⬙ Dive Sites
- ⬿ Beach
- ① Hotels

The Anchorage, **15**

Aqua Bay Club, **18**

Beachcomber, **8**

Caribbean Club, **7**

Christopher Columbus, **16**

Comfort Suites
Grand Cayman, **3**

Coral Stone Club, **10**

Discovery Point Club, **17**

Grand Cayman
Beach Suites, **6**

Grand Cayman
Marriott Beach Resort, **4**

The Grandview, **2**

Harbour View Apartments, **1**

Lacovia Condominiums, **5**

Plantana, **14**

Ritz-Carlton, **11**

Silver Sands, **19**

Sunshine Suites Resort, **9**

Villas of the Galleon, **12**

Westin Grand Cayman
Seven Mile Beach
Resort & Spa, **13**

dining and water-sports facilities; free use of gym (unusual on Grand Cayman); supermarkets and restaurants within walking distance; significant online discounts. **Cons:** most entrances face the street, making it noisy on weekends; small parking lot; several units need refurbishment; music often blaring around the pool. ⑤ *Rooms from: $790 ☒ West Bay Rd., Seven Mile Beach, Grand Cayman ☏ 345/949– 1234 ⊕ www.grand-cayman-beach-suites.com and www. gcbs.ky ⇴ 53 suites ⋈ No meals.*

$$$$ ⊡ **Grand Cayman Marriott Beach Resort.** *Resort.* The soaring, stylish, if impersonal marble lobby (with exquisite art glass, spectacular blown-up underwater photos, and fun elements such as red British-style telephone boxes) sets the tone for this bustling beachfront property. **Pros:** lively bars and restaurants; good snorkeling and water sports; convenient to both George Town and Seven Mile Beach; airport connectivity enables you to print your boarding pass. **Cons:** often overrun by tour groups and conventioneers; narrowest section of Seven Mile Beach; pool and bar often noisy late. ⑤ *Rooms from: $494 ☒ 389 West Bay Rd., Seven Mile Beach, Grand Cayman ☏ 345/949–0088, 800/223–6388 ⊕ www.marriott.com ⇴ 273 rooms, 22 suites ⋈ No meals.*

$$$ ⊡ **The Grandview.** *Rental.* Grand view indeed: all 69 two-
FAMILY and three-bedroom units (sadly only 15 are generally in the rental pool) look smack onto the Caribbean and the beach past splendidly maintained gardens. **Pros:** restaurants and shops within walking distance; wine concierge dispenses advice; free Wi-Fi (when it's available); nice pool and hot tub. **Cons:** the long beach can be rocky; some units a tad worn though meticulously maintained; not all units have access to the free Wi-Fi signal. ⑤ *Rooms from: $475 ☒ 95 Snooze La., Seven Mile Beach, Grand Cayman ☏ 345/945– 4511, 866/977–6766 ⊕ www.grandviewcondos.com ⇴ 69 2- and 3-bedroom condos ⋈ No meals.*

$ ⊡ **Harbour View Apartments.** *Rental.* This little sunshine-yellow enclave delivers on the name's promise, with smashing views of the leviathan cruise ships hulking off George Town. **Pros:** sweet, helpful owners; great value; coin-operated laundry on-site. **Cons:** no pool; rocky small beach (but great snorkeling); dilapidated furnishings. ⑤ *Rooms from: $115 ☒ West Bay Rd., Seven Mile Beach, Grand Cayman ☏ 345/949–5681 ⊕ www.harbourviewapartments.com ⇴ 12 studio and 1-bedroom apartments ⋈ No meals.*

$$$ ⊡ **Lacovia Condominiums.** *Rental.* The carefully manicured courtyard of this handsome arcaded Mediterranean Revival property could easily be mistaken for a peaceful park. **Pros:**

Seven Mile Beach

central location; exquisite gardens; extensive beach. **Cons:** rear courtyard rooms can be noisy from traffic and partying from West Bay Road; pool fairly small (though most people prefer the beach). ⑤ *Rooms from: $415* ✉ *697 West Bay Rd., Seven Mile Beach, Grand Cayman* ☎ *345/949-7599* ⊕ *www. lacovia.com* ⇌ *35 1-, 2-, and 3-bedroom condos* ⦿ *No meals.*

★ **Fodor's**Choice ⌧ **Ritz-Carlton Grand Cayman.** *Resort.* The Ritz-
$$$$ Carlton offers unparalleled luxury and service infused with
FAMILY a welcome sense of place, including works by top local artists and craftspeople. **Pros:** exemplary service; exceptional
facilities with many complimentary extras. **Cons:** annoy-
ingly high per-night resort fee; somewhat sprawling with
a confusing layout; long walk to beach (over an interior
bridge) from most rooms. ⑤ *Rooms from: $659* ✉ *West Bay
Rd., Seven Mile Beach, Grand Cayman* ☎ *345/943-9000*
⊕ *www.ritzcarlton.com* ⇌ *353 rooms, 12 suites, 24 condos*
⦿ *Breakfast.*

$ ⌧ **Sunshine Suites Resort.** *Hotel.* This friendly, all-suites hotel
is an impeccably clean money saver. **Pros:** good value and
Internet deals; cheerful staff; rocking little restaurant;
thoughtful free extras including business center use and
access to the nearby World Gym. **Cons:** poor views; not on
the beach. ⑤ *Rooms from: $234* ✉ *1465 Esterley Tibbetts
Hwy., off West Bay Rd., Seven Mile Beach, Grand Cayman*
☎ *345/949-3000, 877/786-1110* ⊕ *www.sunshinesuites.
com* ⇌ *130 suites* ⦿ *Breakfast.*

Other Lodgings to Consider

Obviously, we can't include every property deserving mention without creating an encyclopedia. Our favorites receive full reviews, but you might consider the following accommodations, many of them equally meritorious.

Beachcomber. Beachcomber rose phoenix-like post-Ivan as a glam high-rise with 40 spacious 2- to 4-bedroom condos (roughly 24 in the rental pool). The decor is high-end, the amenities and appliances high-tech, and there's free underground parking, long-distance calls to North America, and Wi-Fi; HDTV with DVD, a washer/dryer, and a dishwasher. The beach is gorgeous, and the location is ideal (walking distance to groceries and restaurants). It compares favorably to neighbor Caribbean Club. ⊠ *West Bay Rd., Seven Mile Beach, Grand Cayman* ☎ *345/943–6500* ⊕ *www.beachcomber.ky.*

Morritt's Tortuga Club and Resort. Morritt's Tortuga Club and Resort offers 146 well-maintained, fully equipped, mostly time-share units, albeit many lacking beach views and/or access (the best and priciest are branded "Grand Resort"). The more than adequate activities and amenities include the respected Tortuga Divers outfit. It's right next door to the Reef Resort. ⊠ *East End, Grand Cayman* ☎ *345/947–7449, 800/447-0309* ⊕ *www.morritts.com.*

Plantana. Plantana is exceedingly lush, set on a stunning stretch of sand with smashing views of the leviathan ships lumbering into George Town and permeated with the sounds of surf and birdsong. The 49 individually decorated one- to three-bedroom units are fully outfitted (including washer/dryers and Wi-Fi) and handsomely appointed, with designs running from contemporary to colonial, even Asian-inspired. ⊠ *1293 West Bay Rd., Seven Mile Beach, Grand Cayman* ☎ *345/945–4430* ⊕ *www.plantanacayman.com.*

Silver Sands. Silver Sands is an older compound that anchors the quieter northernmost end of Seven Mile Beach, with terrific snorkeling off the spectacular sweep of glittering sand. Most of the 42 cramped units have balconies with fabulous views; second-floor units with vaulted ceilings are preferable. ⊠ *West Bay Rd., Seven Mile Beach, Grand Cayman* ☎ *345/949–3343* ⊕ *www.silversandscondos.com.*

$$$
FAMILY

⌖ **Villas of the Galleon.** *Rental.* On the beachfront, snuggled between the Ritz-Carlton and Westin, Galleon's villas are just steps away from groceries, restaurants, nightlife, and water sports. **Pros:** affable management; central location; glorious beach; free DSL and local calls. **Cons:** no pool; slightly boxy room configuration; one-bedroom units do not have a washer/dryer. ⑤ *Rooms from: $440* ✉ *West Bay Rd., Seven Mile Beach, Grand Cayman* ☏ *345/945–4433, 866/665–4696* ⊕ *www.villasofthegalleon.com* ⇨ *74 1-, 2-, and 3-bedroom condos* ⊙ *No meals.*

★ **Fodor'sChoice** ☲ **Westin Grand Cayman Seven Mile Beach Resort and Spa.** *Resort.* The Westin offers something for everyone, from conventioneers to honeymooners to families, not to mention what the hospitality industry calls "location location location." **Pros:** terrific children's programs; superb beach (the largest resort stretch at 800 feet); better-than-advertised ocean views. **Cons:** occasionally bustling and impersonal when large groups book; daily $35 resort fee. ⑤ *Rooms from: $559* ✉ *West Bay Rd., Seven Mile Beach, Grand Cayman* ☏ *345/945–3800, 800/937–8461* ⊕ *www. westingrandcayman.com* ⇨ *339 rooms, 8 suites* ⊙ *No meals.*

$$$$
FAMILY

WEST BAY

For those who are willing to be out of the thick of things yet who still want fairly close proximity to Seven Mile Beach, there are a handful of resorts and condo rentals available in West Bay. Some of these even have waterfront locations, though they are fronted by ironshore rather than a sandy white beach.

$$ ☲ **Cobalt Coast Resort and Suites.** *Resort.* This small eco-friendly hotel is perfect for divers who want a moderately priced spacious room or suite right on the ironshore far from the madding crowds. **Pros:** superb dive outfit; friendly service and clientele; free Wi-Fi; environmentally aware. **Cons:** poky golden-sand beach; unattractive concrete pool area; remote location, so a car (included in some packages) is necessary. ⑤ *Rooms from: $290* ✉ *18-A Sea Fan Dr., West Bay, Grand Cayman* ☏ *345/946–5656, 888/946–5656* ⊕ *www.cobaltcoast.com* ⇨ *7 rooms, 15 suites* ⊙ *Multiple meal plans.*

★ **Fodor'sChoice** ☲ **Cotton Tree.** *Rental.* Cayman-born owner Heather Lockington has created an authentic haven where guests can embrace Caymanian heritage and reconnect with nature without sacrificing comfort. **Pros:** peaceful and quiet setting; beautifully designed and outfitted accommodations; complimentary airport transfers; wonderful immersion in local culture. **Cons:** luxury comes with a price tag; remote location means a car is required; beach narrow and tangled

$$$$

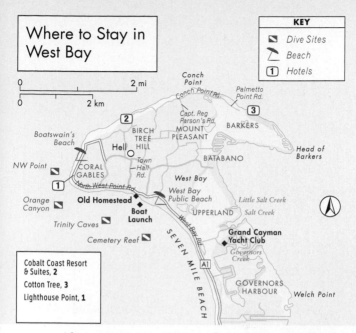

with sea grape trees. ⑤ *Rooms from: $890* ✉ *375 Conch Point Rd., West Bay, Grand Cayman* ☎ *345/943–0700, 561/807–8566 in U.S.* ⊕ *www.caymancottontree.com* 🛏 *4 2-bedroom cottages* ⊗ *Closed Sept.* ❚❘⃝ *No meals.*

★ **Fodor's**Choice ⬚ **Lighthouse Point.** *Resort.* Leading scuba opera-
$$$ tor DiveTech's stunning ecodevelopment features sustainable wood interiors and recycled concrete, an ecosensitive gray-water system, energy-saving appliances and lights, and Cayman's first wind turbine generator. **Pros:** ecofriendly; fantastic shore diving (and state-of-the-art dive shop); creative and often recycled upscale look; superb eatery. **Cons:** no real beach; car necessary; a bit difficult for physically challenged to navigate. ⑤ *Rooms from: $450* ✉ *571 N.W. Point Rd., West Bay, Grand Cayman* ☎ *345/949–1700* ⊕ *www.lighthouse-point-cayman.com* 🛏 *9 2-bedroom apartments* ❚❘⃝ *No meals.*

EAST END

A stay in East End allows you to get away from the crowds and often stay on a lovely, sandy beach.

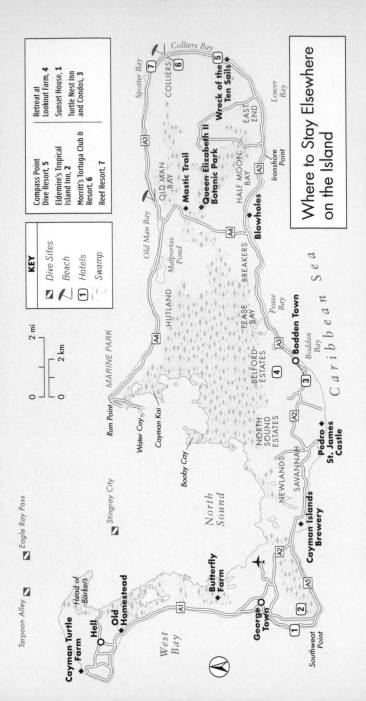

Where to Stay Elsewhere
on the Island

KEY

◢ Dive Sites
⌐ Beach
☐ Hotels
✦ Swamp

Compass Point
Dive Resort, **5**
Eldemire's Tropical
Island Inn, **2**
Moritt's Tortuga Club &
Resort, **6**
Reef Resort, **7**

Retreat at
Lookout Farm, **4**
Sunset House, **1**
Turtle Nest Inn
and Condos, **3**

$$ ☎ **Compass Point Dive Resort.** *Resort.* This tranquil, congenial little getaway run by the admirable Ocean Frontiers scuba operation would steer even nondivers in the right direction. **Pros:** top-notch dive operation; free bike and kayak use; good value especially with packages; affable international staff and clientele. **Cons:** isolated location requires a car; "ecogreen" conservation is admirable but air-conditioning can't go very low. ⑤ *Rooms from: $295* ✉ *Austin Conolly Dr., East End, Grand Cayman* ☎ *345/947–7500, 800/348–6096, 345/947–0000* ⊕ *www.compasspoint.ky* ⤳ *17 1-bedroom, 9 2-bedroom, and 3 3-bedroom condos* ⦿*No meals.*

★ **Fodor's Choice** ☎ **Reef Resort.** *Resort.* This exceedingly well-run
$ time-share property seductively straddles a 600-foot beach on the less hectic East End. **Pros:** romantically remote; glorious beach; enthusiastic staff (including a crackerjack wedding coordinator); great packages. **Cons:** remote; few dining options within easy driving distance; sprawling layout. ⑤ *Rooms from: $270* ✉ *Queen's Hwy., East End, Grand Cayman* ☎ *345/947–3100, 888/232–0541* ⊕ *www. thereef.com* ⤳ *152 suites* ⦿*Multiple meal plans.*

$ ☎ **Retreat at Lookout Farm.** *B&B/Inn.* "Peaceful" is an over-used word, yet it sums up the appeal of this difficult-to-find, back-to-nature hideaway swallowed up in 20 acres of foliage off the main road. **Pros:** utter peace and quiet; genuine Caymanian ambience and warmth; wonderful breakfasts. **Cons:** car needed; no cooking facilities; hard to find and comparatively far from most tourist attractions and top beaches. ⑤ *Rooms from: $149* ✉ *521 Lookout Rd., Bodden Town, Grand Cayman* ☎ *345/947–2386, 705/719–9144* ⊕ *www.retreatatlookout.com* ⤳ *8 rooms* ⦿*Breakfast.*

$ ☎ **Turtle Nest Inn and Condos.** *Rental.* This affordable, intimate, Mediterranean-style seaside inn has roomy one-bedroom apartments and a pool overlooking a narrow beach with good snorkeling. **Pros:** wonderful snorkeling; thoughtful extras; caring staff; free Wi-Fi. **Cons:** car necessary; occasional rocks and debris on beach; ground-floor room views slightly obscured by palms; road noise in back rooms. ⑤ *Rooms from: $149* ✉ *166 Bodden Town Rd., Bodden Town, Grand Cayman* ☎ *345/947–8665* ⊕ *www. turtlenestinn.com, www.turtlenestcondos.com* ⤳ *8 apartments, 10 2-bedroom condos.*

DID YOU KNOW?

More than 40 dive shops take divers to more than 200 individual sites; the Cayman Islands' first dive operation opened in 1957.

GRAND CAYMAN NIGHTLIFE AND PERFORMING ARTS

By Jordan
Simon
Despite Grand Cayman's conservatism and small size, the nightlife scene looms surprisingly large, especially on weekends. Choices include boisterous beach-and-brew hangouts, swanky wine bars, pool halls, sports bars, jammed and jamming dance clubs, live entertainment, and cultural events. A smoking ban was instituted in 2010 for nightspots and restaurants (one preexisting cigar bar and a hookah lounge received special dispensation).

Most major resorts, clubs, and bars offer some kind of performance, including lavish rum-and-reggae limbo/fire-eating/stilt-walking extravaganzas. Local bands with a fan(atic) following include soft-rock duo Hi-Tide; the Pandemonium Steelband; reggae-influenced trio Swanky; hard rockers Ratskyn (who've opened for REO Speedwagon, Mötley Crüe, and Bon Jovi); blues/funk purveyors Madamspeaker; and neo-punk rockers the Blow Holes. Other names to look for are Musical Crew, Sucker Box, Ka, Noel's Band, Wild Knights, Island Vibes, Exit, 45 C.I., Lammie, Heat, Gone Country, and Coco Red.

Consult the "Get Out" section in the Friday edition of the *Caymanian Compass* for listings of live music, movies, theater, and other entertainment. Local magazines such as *Key to Cayman, What's Hot,* and *Destination Cayman* can be picked up free of charge around the island, sometimes providing coupons for discounts and/or freebies. Bars remain open until 1 AM, and clubs are generally open from 10 PM until 3 AM, but they can't serve liquor after midnight on Saturday or permit dancing on Sunday. While shorts and sarongs are usually acceptable attire at beachside bars, smart casual defines the dress code for clubbing.

TIPSY TIPS. Don't drive and drink! Local police set sobriety checkpoints in heavily trafficked areas. The law is strict, the punishment (fine and/or prison) harsh. Revel away: The watering holes will happily pour you into a taxi. Or stick to the walkable cluster of bars in George Town and along Seven Mile Beach. Staggering isn't illegal, just embarrassing.

BEST BETS

■ **A Smokin' Time.** Even if you're not into stogies, Grand Cayman's cigar and wine bars are civilized hangouts where you might see stars or overhear insider trading tips.

■ **Local Rhythms.** Cayman's musicians have fanatic followings; it's worth a trip to The Reef for the hilarious Barefoot Man. Lammie, Coco Red, Karen Edie, Gary Ebanks & Intransit, and Hi-Tide are other memorable musicians.

■ **Fish Feedings.** It's touristy, but watching tarpons pirouet-

ting for bait at sunset reels even locals into waterfront watering holes.

■ **Culture Vultures.** If you want a real feel for Cayman life, take in an original play, particularly such annual special performances and festivals as Rundown and Gimistory.

■ **Full-Moon Parties.** Various beach bars host celebrations with almost pagan abandon, and these parties are overflowing with cocktails and camaraderie.

5

GEORGE TOWN

BARS AND MUSIC CLUBS

Margaritaville. Grand Cayman's Margaritaville is a vast upstairs space that usually bustles with life (especially down its Green Monster waterslide); the Friday-evening happy hour is especially popular, with an overgrown frat-party ambience, and though drinks may be a bit pricier than at other waterfront locations, the jollity, 25 TVs, and free Wi-Fi definitely compensate. It closes early except on Friday nights. ⊠ *Anchorage Center, 32 Harbour Dr., George Town, Grand Cayman* ☎ *345/949–6274* ⊕ *www.margaritavillecaribbean.com* ⊗ *Closed Sun.*

My Bar. This bar is optimally perched on the water's edge, looking almost due west with a perfect vantage point for watching the sunset. The leviathan open-sided cabana is drenched in vivid Rasta colors and crowned by an intricate South Seas–style thatched roof (containing approximately 36,000 palm fronds). Christmas lights and the occasional customer dangle from the rafters year-round. Great grub and a mischievous mix of locals, expats, and tourists from all walks of life prove that ecocentric Cayman offers wild life alongside the wildlife. ⊠ *Sunset House, S. Church St., George Town, Grand Cayman* ☎ *345/949–7111* ⊕ *www.sunsethouse.com.*

Rackam's Waterfront Pub and Restaurant. A Cayman mosaic of fishermen to Who's-the-Hugo-Boss financiers savors sensational sunsets followed by exuberantly pirouetting tarpon feeding at the open-air, marine-theme happenin' bar built on a jetty jutting into the harbor (boaters, even snorkelers cruise right up the ladder for drinks while anglers leave their catch on ice) that has complimentary snacks on Friday and serves pub fare at fair prices until midnight. ⊠ *93 N. Church St., George Town, Grand Cayman* ☎ *345/945–3860* ⊕ *www.rackams.com.*

The Wharf. You can dance near the water to mellow music on Saturday evenings; when there's a wedding reception in the pavilion, the crashing surf and candles twinkling as if competing with the stars bathe the proceedings in an almost Gatsby-esque glow. For something less sedate, Roger and Sarah conduct sizzling salsa dancing and lessons on Tuesdays after dinner, while most Fridays morph into a wild 1970s disco night (after free hors d'oeuvres during the joyous happy hour). The stunning seaside setting on tiered decks compensates for often undistinguished food and service. The Ports of Call bar is a splendid place for sunset fanciers, and tarpon feeding off the deck is a nightly 9 pm spectacle. ⊠ *West Bay Rd., George Town, Grand Cayman* ☎ *345/949–2231.*

SEVEN MILE BEACH

BARS AND MUSIC CLUBS
The Attic. The Attic is a chic sports bar with three billiard tables, classic arcade games (Space Invaders, Donkey Kong), air hockey, and large-screen TVs (you can nab a private booth with its own flat-panel job). Events encompass daily happy hours, trivia nights, and the Caribbean's reputedly largest Bloody Mary bar on Sunday. Along with downstairs sister hot spot "O" Bar, it's ground zero for the Wednesday Night Drinking Club. For a $25 initiation fee (you get a T-shirt and personalized leather wristband, toga optional) and $10 weekly activity fee, you'll be shuttled by bus to several different bars, with free shots and drinks specials all night. ⊠ *Queen's Court, 2nd fl., West Bay Rd., Seven Mile Beach, Grand Cayman* ☎ *345/949–7665* ⊕ *www.obar. attic.ky.*

Calico Jack's. For a casual drink, visit this friendly outdoor beach bar at the north end of the public beach with a DJ on Saturday and open-mike night on Tuesday, bands many

Caymans Captivating Carnival

Held annually during the first week of May (or the week after Easter), the four-day **Batabano Cayman Carnival** (⊕ www. caymancarnival.com) is the island's boisterous answer to Mardi Gras, not to mention Carnival in Rio and Trinidad. Though not as hedonistic, the pyrotechnic pageantry, electricity, and enthralled throngs are unrivaled (except for during Pirates Week). Events include a carnival ball, soca and calypso song competitions, massive Mas (masquerade) parade with ornate floats, street dance, and a beach fete. The festivities are enhanced by tasty concession stands offering Caymanian and other Caribbean cuisine and delicacies.

The word *batabano* refers to the tracks that turtles leave as they heave onto beaches to nest. Locating those tracks was reason to celebrate in the olden times, when turtling was a major part of the economy, so it seemed an appropriate tribute to the islands' heritage, alongside the traditional Caribbean celebration of the region's African roots. Indeed, many of the increasingly elaborate costumes are inspired by Cayman's majestic marine life and maritime history from parrots to pirates, though some offer provocative social commentary. Thousands of revelers line the streets each year cheering their favorite masqueraders and boogying to the Mas steel pan and soca bands. The organizers also hold a stand-alone street parade for Cayman's youth called Junior Carnival Batabano the weekend before the adult parade. Equally exciting, it stresses the importance of teaching students the art of costume making and Mas, ensuring Carnival won't become another dying Caymanian custom.

Friday nights, and riotous parties during the full moon when even Ritz-Carlton guests let their hair and inhibitions down. ⊠ *West Bay Rd., Seven Mile Beach, Grand Cayman* ☎ *345/945–7850*.

Coconut Joe's. You can sit at the bar or swing under a century-old poinciana tree and watch the traffic go by. There are murals of apes everywhere, from gorillas doing shots to a baboon in basketball uniform (in keeping with management's facetious suggestion that you attract your server's attention by pounding your chest while screeching and scratching yourself). It's particularly popular with the younger tourism- and hospitality-industry crowds (ply them with beers for some hair- and eyebrow-raising backstage stories). Friday really swings with DJs and free happy-hour munchies. ✉ *Across from Comfort Suites, West Bay Rd., Seven Mile Beach, Grand Cayman* ☎ *345/943–5637* ⊕ *www. coconutjoecayman.com.*

Deckers. Always bustling and bubbly, Deckers takes its name from the red English double-decker bus that forms the focal point of the main outdoor bar. You can luxuriate indoors on cushy sofas over a chess game and signature blood-orange mojito; hack your way through the 18-hole safari miniature-golf course; find a secluded nook in the garden terrace framed by towering palms, old-fashioned ornate street lamps, and colonial columns; or groove Thursday through Saturday nights to the easy-listening potpourri of pop, reggae, blues, and country courtesy of the Hi-Tide duo. Worthy Carib-Mediterranean fusion cuisine is a bonus (try the Caribbean lobster mac n' cheese or the coconut shrimp with citrus marmalade and green papaya salad). ✉ *West Bay Rd., Seven Mile Beach, Grand Cayman* ☎ *345/945–6600* ⊕ *www.deckers.ky.*

Duke's Seafood & Rib Shack. Duke's offers the ultimate in beach shack chic (albeit a half block back from the sand), from the awesome surfing photos to the reclaimed drift-wood patio bar to the statue of the big kahuna with shades and board atop a manta ray. Locals and visitors alike belly up to the raw and real bars, especially during nightly happy hours, to soak up "Cayman's endless summer." ✉ *West Bay Rd. across from Public Beach, Seven Mile Beach, Grand Cayman* ☎ *345/640–0000* ⊕ *www.dukescayman.com.*

Fidel Murphy's Irish Pub. This pub has an unusual logo, a stogie-smoking Castro surrounded by shamrocks. Indeed, the congenial Irish wit and whimsy are so thick that you half expect to find Fidel and Gerry Adams harping on U.S. and U.K. policy over a Harp. The pub's Edwardian decor of etched glass, hardwood, and brass may be prefabricated (it was constructed in Ireland, disassembled, and shipped), but everything else is genuine, from the warm welcome to the ales and cider on tap to the proper Irish stew (though the kitchen also turns out conch fritters and chicken tandoori wraps). Sunday and Monday host all-you-can-eat extravaganzas (fish-and-chips, carvery) at rock-bottom prices. Trivia nights and live music lure regulars through the week. Weekends welcome live televised Gaelic soccer, rugby, and hurling, followed by karaoke and *craic* (if you go, you'll learn the definition soon enough). ✉ *Queen's*

Calling All Corsairs

For 11 days in November, Grand Cayman is transformed into a nonstop, fun-filled festivity every bit as flamboyant as Johnny Depp's Jack Sparrow performances. The annual **Pirates Week Festival** (⊕ www. piratesweekfestival.com) is the country's largest celebration, encompassing more than 30 different events, including street dances, five heritage days (where various districts showcase their unique craft and culinary traditions), a float parade, landing pageant, fireworks, song contests, costume competitions, cardboard-boat regattas, golf tournaments, swim meets, autocross, races, kids' fun day, teen music nights, underwater treasure hunt, and more.

Everyone gets involved in the high-spirited high jinks (for example, dive boats stage mock battles and play practical jokes like filling the decks of "rivals" with cornflakes or jam, while swashbucklers "capture" hotel employees and guests). The opening night is an explosion of sights and sounds, from fireworks to rocking, rollicking bands that keep thousands shaking booty in the George Town streets into the wee hours of the morning. Later in the week, another highlight is the mock pirate invasion of Hog Sty Bay and the spirited defense of the capital, culminating in the buccaneers' trial and extravagantly costumed street parades with ornate floats.

Most of the major events are free. The music sizzles, and the evening functions feature heaping helpings of yummy, affordable local fare (turtle stew, conch, jerk chicken). Given the enormous popularity of the festival, travelers should make reservations for hotel rooms and rental cars well in advance. Even taxis are in short supply for those wanting to attend the farther-flung heritage days. Hotels, shops, and the festival's administrative office do a brisk biz in corsair couture (though you can bring your own stuffed parrot and patch; just leave the sword at home).

Court, West Bay Rd., Seven Mile Beach, Grand Cayman ☎*345/949–5189.*

Legendz. A sports bar with a clubby, retro feel (Marilyn Monroe and Frank Sinatra photos channel the glamour days, while scarlet booths and bubble chandeliers add oomph), it's the usual testosterone test drive with plentiful scoring of both types. Good luck wrestling a spot at the bar for Pay-Per-View and major live sporting events (though 10 TVs, including two 6-by-8 foot, high-resolution screens broadcast to every corner). It doubles as an entertainment venue, booking local bands, stand-up comics, and leading island DJs. You can also savor grilled fare at fair prices. ✉ *Falls Centre, West Bay Rd., Seven Mile Beach, Grand Cayman.*

Lone Star Bar and Grill. The bar and restaurant proudly calls itself Cayman's top dive (and indeed, locals from dive masters to dentists get down and occasionally dirty over kick-ass margaritas). The noisy bar glorifies sports, Texas, and the boob tube, from murals of Cowboys cheerleaders to an amazing sports memorabilia collection (including items signed by both Bushes), and 17 big-screen TVs tuned to different events. ✉ *686 West Bay Rd., Seven Mile Beach, Grand Cayman* ☎ *345/945–5175* ⊕ *www.lonestar cayman.com.*

Stingers Resort and Pool Bar. Stingers Resort and Pool Bar offers tasty affordable food in an appealing setting (check out the stupendous "stinger" mosaic), with cover-free live music and dancing Thursday and Friday. Wednesday nights there's a very affordable all-you-can-eat Caribbean luau. The band Heat, a local institution, sizzles with energetic, emotionally delivered calypso, reggae, soca, salsa, and oldies; then the limbo dancers and fire-eaters keep the temperature rising. If you recoil from audience participation, stay far away. More exhibitionistic "spring break" sorts might find their photo adorning the "Wall of Shame," but the worst blackmail is persuading you to buy another blue-green Stingers punch. ✉ *Comfort Suites, West Bay Rd., Seven Mile Beach, Grand Cayman* ☎ *345/945–3000* ⊕ *www.stingersrestaurantandbar.com.*

CIGAR AND WINE LOUNGES

Nectar. Don't let the location of Nectar, which is in the back of a plain strip mall, fool you. This is a chic New York–style martini lounge and sushi bar with a tapestry of tapas on tap and more than 30 different drinks—including many tinis with tude. Choose from bar, tall tables, or sofas in the sleek, slick, mostly monochrome space with chrome accents, blue seats, and red lighting. There's new art on the walls every month, special shisha (hookah) evenings, and DJs spinning Sexy Fridays and Tropical Saturdays, when it becomes a slim-hipper-than-thou club that delivers a dancing high for Jessica Alba wannabes poured into spandex and Gap poster-boy slackers (potential hell for anyone over

CLOSE UP

Barefoot Man

H. George Nowak, aka "Barefoot Man," is hardly your ordinary Calypsonian. The blond-haired German-born, self-described "Nashville musical reject" moved from Munich to North Carolina after his mother remarried an Air Force officer. But "the inveterate map lover" dreamed of island life.

He started his island-hopping career in the U.S. Virgin Islands, then Hawaii, then the Bahamas ("the smaller, less populated, the better"), finally settling in the Cayman Islands in 1971. "'But there's nothing there,' people said. I replied, 'That's the point!'" Needless to say, Barefoot prefers the casual lifestyle.

He quickly realized that the audience "didn't want 'Folsom Prison Blues,' they wanted 'Banana Boat Song.'" He was dubbed Barefoot Boy ("since the nicest pair of footwear I owned were my Voit diving flippers") in 1971. While he'll still throw in a country or blues tune, Barefoot came to love the calypso tradition, especially its double entendres and political commentary. His witty ditties say it all: "Thong Gone Wrong," "Ship Faced," "The Gay Cruise Ship Song," and "Save the Lap Dance for Me."

One of the most passionate, outspoken, articulate expats on the subject of sustainable tourism, he wittily rants in song and print (including his own self-published *Fun News,* the überglossy coffee-table *Grand Cayman* magazine, and hilarious tomes like *Which Way to the Islands?*). "I've seen the island go from three taxi drivers to, I think, 380 in the taxi association...saw how the first high-rise, the former Holiday Inn, changed Cayman irrevocably in the '70s.... I compare tourism to aspirin—a couple are okay, but take the whole bottle, you die," he jokes (mostly).

He'll regale you between sets or over beers with colorful (expletive deleted) anecdotes of island life, recounting adventures from a bogus murder charge in the Bahamas to the necessity of scheduling spliff breaks when recording in Jamaica to being mistaken for a DEA agent.

Barefoot sums up his philosophy simply and eloquently in one of his most popular lyrics (add gentle reggae-ish lilt), "I wish I were a captain, Sailin' on the sea. I'd sail out to an island, Take you there with me. I'd throw away the compass, Oh what a dirty scheme.... Someday I might wake up, realize where I am, dreamin' like some 10-year-old, out in Disneyland, There is no tomorrow when you're living in a dream."

5

30 years old or 20% body fat). ⊠ *Seven Mile Shops, Seven Mile Beach, Grand Cayman* ☎ *345/949–1802.*

Silver Palm Lounge. The Silver Palm drips with cash and cachet, with a model waitstaff and chic clientele. One section faithfully replicates a classic English country library (perfect for civilized, proper afternoon tea or a pre- or post-dinner champagne or single malt). The other forms Taikun, a sensuous sushi spot clad mostly in black, with a popular public table. Also on tap: fab cocktails, including specialty martinis (the Silver Palm cosmopolitan is a winner—Ketel One citron, triple sec, a squeeze of fresh lime juice, and a splash of cranberry topped off with Moët champagne); pages of wines by the glass; and an impressive list of cigars, cognacs, and aged drums. ⊠ *Ritz-Carlton, West Bay Rd., Seven Mile Beach, Grand Cayman* ☎ *345/943–9000.*

West Indies Wine Store. This is an ultra-contemporary wine store with a difference: You purchase tasting cards, allowing you to sample any of the 80-odd wines and even spirits available by the sip, half- or full glass via the argon-enhanced "intelligent dispensing system." Selections traverse a vast canny range of prices, regions, styles, and terroirs. "We slot in well-known labels so you don't feel lost, but also stay relatively obscure on beers, ales, and ciders for fun," notes manager Alex McClenaghan. Even better, the enterprising owners struck a deal with neighboring restaurants and gourmet shops to provide appetizers or cheese and charcuterie plates, best savored alfresco at the tables in front of the handsome space. Small wonder savvy locals congregate here after work or movies at the nearby cineplex. ⊠ *Corner of Market St. and The Paseo, Camana Bay, Grand Cayman* ☎ *345/640–9492* ⊕ *www.wiwc.ky.*

DANCE CLUBS
"O" Bar. "O" Bar is a trendy black-and-crimson, industrial-style dance club with mixed music (live on Saturdays) and juggling, flame-throwing bartenders—practically local celebs—flipping cocktails with cojones every night. It's as close to a stand-and-pose milieu as you'll find on Cayman, with the occasional fashion fascist parading in Prada. An upper-level private loft is available by reservation. ⊠ *Queen's Court, West Bay Rd., Seven Mile Beach, Grand Cayman* ☎ *345/943–6227* ⊕ *www.obar.attic.ky.*

Preserving Caymans Cultural Heritage

Several worthy organizations are dedicated to keeping Caymanian traditions alive, including the National Trust of the Cayman Islands, which restores historic buildings and offers craft demonstrations and talks. The Cayman National Cultural Foundation mounts storytelling, musical, dance, and theatrical presentations, as well as readings and art exhibits that respect the "old ways" while seeking new forms of expression. The National Gallery also seeks to ensure vibrant vital world-class artistic development.

Respected local artist Chris Christian (who curates the Ritz-Carlton Gallery exhibits), co-founded **Cayman Traditional Arts** (CTA ⊠ 60 W. Church St., West Bay ☎ 345/946–0117

⊕ artcayman.blogspot.com), which offers interactive classes for children and adults interested in learning authentic Caymanian arts, crafts, and recipes: Thatch weaving, kite making, gig making and spinning, rope making, and an old-style cook-out on the wood-burning oven called a caboose are just some of the topics. The network of freelance artisans has practiced these traditional crafts and customs their entire lives, often handed down over several generations, and represent the best in their disciplines. You really get hands-on in CTA's "living museum" headquarters, a 1917 mauve-and-mint wattle-and-daub cottage with ironwood posts that also doubles as a studio for Chris and Carly Jackson. It's a unique interactive immersion in local culture.

WEST BAY

BARS AND MUSIC CLUBS

Macabuca Oceanside Tiki Bar. A classic hip-hopping happening beach bar, Macabuca has a huge deck over the water, thatched roof, amazing Asian-inspired mosaic murals of waves, spectacular sunsets (and sunset-colored libations), and tiki torches illuminating the reef fish come evening. Macabuca means "What does it matter?" in the indigenous Antillean Taíno language, perfectly encapsulating the mellow vibe. Big-screen TVs, live bands and DJs on weekends, excellent pub grub, and daily specials (CI$7 jerk dishes weekends; Monday all-night happy hour, DJ, and CI$15 all-you-can-eat barbecue) lure everyone from well-heeled loafers to barefoot bodysurfers animatedly discussing current events and dive currents in a Babel of

tongues. ⊠ *Northwest Point Rd., West Bay, Grand Cayman*
☎ *345/945–5217* ⊕ *www.crackedconch.com.ky.*

BARS AND MUSIC CLUBS

Rusty Pelican. This spot draws an eclectic group of dive masters, expats, honeymooners, and mingling singles. The knockout, colorful cocktails pack quite a punch, making the sunset last for hours. The bar dialogue is entertainment enough, but don't miss local legend, country-Calypsonian Barefoot Man, when he plays "upstairs" at Pelican's Reef— he's to Cayman what Jimmy Buffett is to Key West. ⊠ *Reef Resort, Colliers, East End, Grand Cayman* ☎ *345/947– 3100* ⊕ *www.thereef.com.*

South Coast Bar and Grill. South Coast Bar and Grill is a delightful seaside slice of old Cayman (grizzled regulars slamming down dominoes, fabulous sea views, old model cars, Friday-night dances to local legend Lammie's beats, karaoke Saturdays with local Elvis impersonator Errol Dunbar, and reasonably priced local eats like red conch chowder and jerk chicken sausage). It's also a big politico hangout ("that big shark mural ain't just about nature," one bartender cackled), attested to by the fascinating photos, some historical, of local scenes and personalities. The juke jives, from Creedence Clearwater Revival to Mighty Sparrow. ⊠ *Breakers, East End, Grand Cayman* ☎ *345/947–2517* ⊕ *www.southcoastbar.com.*

PERFORMING ARTS

Grand Cayman mounts special events throughout the year. The Cayman National Orchestra performs in disparate venues from the Cracked Conch restaurant to First Baptist Church. There's a burgeoning theater scene. Many new works use religious themes as a launching pad for meditations on issues relevant to current events, such as the Cayman Drama Society (⊕ *www.caymandrama.org.ky*), which put on a provocative offering, *The Judith Code*, updating the biblical heroine's story to a present-day London of TV talk-show hosts and terrorist coalitions; the company also produces stimulating children's fare (*Mort*, based on Terry Pratchett's *Discworld* novels about a young boy apprenticed to Death), as well as escapist crowd-pleasing revivals like *Hairspray* and *Godspell*.

TELLING TALES. The Cayman National Cultural Foundation started "Gimistory" as a means of preserving the rich but vanishing oral-

The Lowdown on Rundown

Rundown is a steamy Caymanian fish stew combining a potpourri of ingredients. A rundown is also a quick summary, and this enduringly popular show performed annually in October since 1991 puns on both definitions. The format is a series of skits, music, stand-up comedy, monologues, cabaret, dance, and impersonations—written from scratch each year by playwright-actor Dave Martins: a light-hearted, topical, satirical lampoon of daily Caymanian life, current events, politics, personalities, and nationalities. Caymanians call it their answer to *The Daily Show* and *Colbert Report*.

Martins started Rundown because he'd "seen topical shows in other Caribbean countries... and felt something similar would work here, but Cayman is very conservative and people said that would get me in hot water." After seeing caricatures of prominent people hanging in their offices, "I concluded that Caymanians were ready to laugh at themselves and wrote the first show. Some of the cast were very apprehensive in rehearsals, but it was a hit from day one." Every year provides fodder and inspiration aplenty,

but the show is more gently mocking than controversial, and the targets of its barbs usually laugh along with everyone else.

The audience's nonstop guffawing may bemuse tourists. Martins explains, "A lot of the stuff I write... is very contextual and almost always local, so the lyrics generally make little sense to someone outside that frame." Recent skits spoofed the red tape involved in putting up a little backyard shed to play dominoes; interplay among a crowd of people lining up to get Caymanian Immigration Status (the rollover policy); a Jamaican trying to teach a Londoner to speak the J dialect; and a lost tourist trying to get directions from a group that includes a Cuban, a Barbadian, a Pakistani, a Jamaican, a Chinaman, and, of course, a Caymanian... "all of whom are incomprehensible to the visitor.... To understand it fully, you'd need to have lived here 10, 15 years." He doesn't Americanize or clean up the dialect, but that augments the honest authenticity. And much of the material, from frustrating daily interactions to bureaucratic blundering, transcends any cultural divide.

culture tradition once passed from generation to generation. Held annually the last week of November, it features storytellers, often in elaborate garb, from Cayman and the Caribbean "spinnin' yarn" about old-time legends (duppies, spirits who return as bogeymen; or Pierrot Grande, the clown dressed in a colorful patchwork quilt of rags) as well as their travels and experiences. Free admission includes Caymanian delicacies like conch fritters and swanky (lemonade), part of a culinary competition.

VENUES

Harquail Theatre. This state-of-the-art facility seats 330 for theatrical performances, concerts, dance recitals, fashion shows, beauty pageants, art exhibits, and poetry readings sponsored by the Cayman National Cultural Foundation. ✉ *17 Harquail Dr., George Town, Grand Cayman* ☎ *345/949–5477.*

Lions Centre. The center hosts events throughout the year: "Battle of the Bands" competitions, concerts by top names on the Caribbean and international music scene such as Maxi Priest, stage productions, pageants, and sporting events. ✉ *Harquail Dr., Red Bay, Grand Cayman* ☎ *345/945–4667, 345/949–7211.*

Prospect Playhouse. A thrust proscenium stage allows the Cayman Drama Society and its partner arts organizations to mount comedies, musicals, and dramas (original and revival) year-round. ✉ *223B Shamrock Rd., Prospect, Grand Cayman* ☎ *345/947–1998, 345/949–5054.*

GRAND CAYMAN SPORTS AND OUTDOOR ACTIVITIES

With Beaches

By Jordan Simon

Water, water, and still more water rippling from turquoise to tourmaline; and underneath lies nature's even more kaleidoscopically colorful answer to Disney World for scuba divers and snorkelers. The Cayman Islands' early aggressive efforts on behalf of marine conservation paid off by protecting some of the most spectacular reefs in the Western Hemisphere. There are innumerable ways to experience their pyrotechnics without getting your feet or hair wet, from submarines to remote-controlled robots, not to mention a bevy of other water sports from windsurfing to wrangling big-game fish, parasailing to paddling kayaks through mangrove swamps.

While most activities on Grand Cayman are aquatic in nature, landlubbers can do more than just loll on the lovely beaches. There are nature hikes, bird-watching treks, and horseback rides through the island's wilder, more remote areas. The golf scene is well above par for so small an island, with courses designed by Jack "The Golden Bear" Nicklaus and, fittingly, "The White Shark" Greg Norman. Even the most seasoned sea salts might enjoy terra firma, at least for half a day.

BEACHES

Grand Cayman is blessed with many fine beaches, ranging from cramped, untrammeled coves to long stretches basking like a cat in the sun, lined with bustling bars and watersports concessions. All beaches are public, though access can be restricted by resorts. Remember that the Cayman Islands are a conservative place: Nudity is strictly forbidden and punishable by a hefty fine and/or prison time.

GEORGE TOWN AND ENVIRONS

Smith's Cove. South of the Grand Old House, this tiny but popular protected swimming and snorkeling spot makes a wonderful beach wedding location. The bottom drops off quickly enough to allow you to swim and play close to shore. Although slightly rocky (its pitted limestone boulders resemble Moore sculptures), there's little debris and few coral heads, plenty of shade, picnic tables, restrooms, and parking. Surfers will find decent swells just to the south. Note the curious obelisk cenotaph "In memory of James Samuel Webster and his wife Arabella Antoinette (née Eden)," with assorted quotes from Confucius to John Donne. **Amenities:** parking; toilets. **Best for:** snorkeling;

BEST BETS

■ **A Ray-diant Experience.** Feeding and stroking the silky denizens of Stingray City and Stingray Sandbar are highlights of any Cayman trip.

■ **Snorkeling or Diving from Shore.** Whether you make it to Stingray City or even scuba dive, you're all wet if you don't check out the pyrotechnic reef life glittering just offshore.

■ **Hiking the Mastic Trail.** The ecocentric should hike (and sometimes hack their way) through this mix of ecosystems, including ancient dry forest that embraces 716 plant species as well as (harmless) wildlife.

■ **ROV-ing the Ocean's Depths.** Deep See Cayman's ROV robot explores 2,000 feet under the sea while you watch in comfort on a yacht; the kids can steer if they're handy with joysticks.

■ **Putting on the Nightlights.** Kayak when the moon is waning to a bioluminescent bay; millions of microorganisms glow like fireflies when disturbed.

6

sunset; swimming. ⊠ *Off S. Church St., George Town, Grand Cayman.*

South Sound Cemetery Beach. A narrow, sandy driveway takes you past the small cemetery to a perfect beach. The dock here is primarily used by dive boats during winter storms. You can walk in either direction; the sand is talcum-soft and clean, the water calm and clear (though local surfers take advantage of occasional small reef breaks; if wading, wear reef shoes, since the bottom is somewhat rocky and dotted with sea urchins). You'll definitely find fewer crowds. **Amenities:** none. **Best for:** solitude; surfing. ⊠ *S. Sound Rd., Prospect, Grand Cayman.*

SEVEN MILE BEACH

★ **Fodor's**Choice **Seven Mile Beach.** Grand Cayman's west coast is dominated by the famous Seven Mile Beach—actually a 6½-mile-long (10-km-long) expanse of powdery white sand overseeing lapis water stippled with a rainbow of parasails and kayaks. Free of litter and pesky peddlers, it's an unspoiled (though often crowded) environment. Most of the island's resorts, restaurants, and shopping centers sit along this strip. The public beach toward the north end offers chairs for rent ($10 for the day, including a beverage), a playground, water toys aplenty, beach

DID YOU KNOW?

Rum Point offers excellent snorkeling and soft sand along the North Sound, which is protected by a reef, so there are few waves here.